Men-at-Arms • 448

Irish-American Units in the Civil War

Thomas G. Rodgers • Illustrated by Richard Hook

Series editor Martin Windrow

First published in Great Britain in 2008 by Osprey Publishing
Midland House, West Way, Botley, Oxford, OX2 0PH, UK
443 Park Avenue South, New York, NY 10016, USA
E-mail: info@ospreypublishing.com

A CIP catalog record for this book is available from the British Library

ISBN: 978 1 84603 326 1

Edited by Martin Windrow
Page layout by Alan Hamp
Index by Glyn Sutcliffe
Typeset in New Baskerville and Helvetica
Originated by PPS Grasmere Ltd
Printed in China through World Print Ltd

08 09 10 11 12   10 9 8 7 6 5 4 3 2 1

FOR A CATALOG OF ALL BOOKS PUBLISHED BY
OSPREY MILITARY AND AVIATION PLEASE CONTACT:

NORTH AMERICA
Osprey Direct, c/o Random House Distribution Center
400 Hahn Road, Westminster, MD 21157
E-mail: info@ospreydirect.com

ALL OTHER REGIONS
Osprey Direct UK, P.O. Box 140 Wellingborough, Northants, NN8 2FA, UK
E-mail: info@ospreydirect.co.uk

Osprey Publishing is supporting the Woodland Trust, the UK's leading
woodland conservation charity, by funding the dedication of trees.

www.ospreypublishing.com

Artist's note

Readers may care to note that the original paintings from which the
color plates in this book were prepared are available for private
sale. All reproduction copyright whatsoever is retained by the
Publishers. All inquiries should be addressed to:

Richard Hook
PO Box 475, Hailsham, East Sussex BN27 2SL, UK

The Publishers regret that they can enter into no correspondence
upon this matter.

IRISH-AMERICAN UNITS IN THE CIVIL WAR

IRISH IMMIGRATION

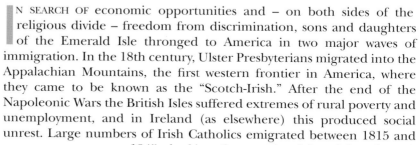

BrigGen Thomas Francis Meagher, the Irish-born soldier and nationalist who was the guiding force behind the Irish Brigade of the Army of the Potomac. In this image Meagher wears the uniform of a brigadier-general; and note the gold braid band on his kepi. (Library of Congress)

N SEARCH OF economic opportunities and – on both sides of the religious divide – freedom from discrimination, sons and daughters of the Emerald Isle thronged to America in two major waves of immigration. In the 18th century, Ulster Presbyterians migrated into the Appalachian Mountains, the first western frontier in America, where they came to be known as the "Scotch-Irish." After the end of the Napoleonic Wars the British Isles suffered extremes of rural poverty and unemployment, and in Ireland (as elsewhere) this produced social unrest. Large numbers of Irish Catholics emigrated between 1815 and 1845, looking for rough pick-and-shovel work in the booming American canal- and railroad-building industries, and the disastrous Potato Famine drove another million and a half of them across the Atlantic between 1845 and 1854. By far the majority settled in Northern cities such as Boston, New York and Chicago, but Southern seaports and river towns – particularly Memphis, New Orleans and Savannah – also witnessed dramatic increases in their Irish populations.

While the majority of immigrants found work in unskilled jobs, budding Irish entrepreneurs set up small shops, grocery stores, taverns, hotels and boardinghouses. Irish professionals made their mark in journalism, education and politics. Cities including Boston, New York, Charleston and New Orleans came to have heavily Irish police forces. The new immigrants established distinctly Irish neighborhoods in America, with strong family and community bonds and stalwart ties to the Catholic Church. They also maintained contacts with the land of their birth, and an ongoing involvement in Irish political and revolutionary causes.

It was middle-class Irish who took the lead in organizing volunteer militia companies in the larger American cities. These companies drilled, engaged in shooting matches, and sponsored balls and banquets, all of which provided important social outlets for the immigrants. Enlisted members often came from the poor laboring class, while officers were usually young sons of the Irish-American professional and

Volunteer militia officers of the Irish Brigade of New York are depicted here in 1852. Units represented include (left to right) the Irish Volunteers, Napper Tandy Light Artillery, Montgomery Guard, Brigade Lancers and Irish Dragoons. (Library of Congress)

Members of the Union army's Irish Brigade in mostly civilian dress in Virginia, summer 1862. This group of officers includes chaplains Father William Corby (seated right) and Father James Dillon (center). (Library of Congress)

merchant class. Nearly every large American city had at least one Irish volunteer military company, and some – New York, Chicago, Boston and New Orleans – boasted many.

Militia companies both encouraged American patriotism and boosted Irish pride. Green uniforms, and the generous use of Irish war mottoes and symbols such as the shamrock and the harp, were common. The immigrants often named their companies after Irish national heroes like Robert Emmet, Daniel O'Connell and Patrick Sarsfield, as well as Andrew Jackson (many regarded "Old Hickory" as the first Irish-American president). They paraded on St Patrick's Day as well as on Independence Day and other patriotic occasions.

THE UNION IRISH

Some 150,000 Irish immigrants served in the Union army during the Civil War. In the North, Irish immigrants genuinely saw military service as a way to demonstrate their loyalty to their new homeland, but many were also faced with the unattractive choice between military service and poor civilian employment opportunities. Irish Americans fought to preserve the Union, but many also saw the war as a training ground for another armed struggle to come – a war of Irish liberation from Britain. New York by far outdistanced all other American cities in the number of Irish-American military companies formed both before and during the Civil War. With more than 200,000 Irish (a quarter of the city's population) at the outbreak of war, this metropolis accounted for a third of the total number of Irishmen who served in the Federal army.

The famous Irish Brigade in the Army of the Potomac was the most visibly ethnic command of Irish Americans. Formed in the fall of 1861 with the famous "Fighting 69th" New York as its nucleus, and commanded by popular Irish-American nationalist Thomas Francis Meagher, the Irish Brigade also included the 63rd and 88th New York Infantry Regiments, later joined by the 28th Massachusetts and 116th Pennsylvania. A source of pride to Irish Americans throughout the North, the Irish Brigade suffered very heavy losses at Antietam and Fredericksburg in September and December 1862.

There were other large Irish-American Federal units apart from this formation. A second Irish brigade, Corcoran's Irish Legion, was formed in the western part of New York state. Other Irish commands from the Empire State were the 20th New York State Militia (Ulster Guard), and the 37th New York (Irish Rifles). The Irish in New England were well represented in the 9th Connecticut, 9th Massachusetts, and 10th New Hampshire infantry regiments. From the Keystone State came the 69th and 116th Pennsylvania. Irishmen from the Midwest served in the 10th Ohio (Montgomery Regiment), 23rd and 90th Illinois, 35th Indiana and 17th Wisconsin. From west of the Mississippi came the "Irish 7th" Missouri and 30th Missouri (Shamrock Regiment). In addition to these identifiably Irish units, large numbers of Irish Americans served individually in the regular US Army, and many more in volunteer units enlisted from right across the Northern states.

Connecticut

Cities such as New Haven, Bridgeport and Waterbury became homes to sizeable Irish immigrant populations in the early part of the 19th century. Large numbers of Irishmen enlisted in the 9th Connecticut Infantry Regiment ("Irish Regiment"), organized at New Haven in September 1861. By the end of that fall the regiment had been transported to the Gulf coast, and by the following spring to New Orleans.

During the hottest part of summer 1862 the 9th Connecticut was assigned to the "Williams Canal" operation, an unsuccessful Federal project to divert the course of the Mississippi river and bypass Confederate guns at Vicksburg. The lack of safe drinking water, shortages of supplies and sweltering heat (with temperatures soaring to 115°F) quickly took a toll in casualties, and the regiment lost 153 men to malaria and dysentery. (This use of Irish labor by the Federals proved an ironic parallel to the South's use of Irish immigrants for canal-building – work considered too dangerous for valuable slaves.) At Baton Rouge on August 5, 1862, the 9th Connecticut's Col Thomas M. Cahill (formerly captain of the Emmet Guard of New Haven) took command of the Federal troops after the death of BrigGen Thomas Williams, and successfully repelled a Confederate assault.

In 1864 the Irish Regiment served in Virginia; on October 19, during Jubal Early's offensive in the Shenandoah Valley, the 9th Connecticut played a prominent part in the Federal victory at Cedar Creek, snatched by Phil Sheridan from apparently certain defeat. The regiment was the first to plant its colors on the captured Rebel works, losing only 30 men killed and wounded. The 9th Connecticut carried a distinctive dark blue regimental flag that combined traditional Irish symbols with the American eagle and flag. The eagle sat atop two shields: the US stars and stripes, and an Irish green shield with a central gold harp, above a riband proclaiming *Erin Go Bragh* ("Ireland Forever"). The other side of the flag bore the Connecticut state seal.

Lack of clothing and equipment was a problem for the 9th Connecticut in its early days. The regiment was indifferently uniformed in shoddy blue clothing when first mustered in, and was without arms until December 1861, when it received Enfield rifles at Ship Island off the Mississippi coast. Lieutenant-Colonel John G. Healy reported that the Irishmen were "wretchedly clad," many of the soldiers being without

Many Irish-American regiments carried both the US national flag and a regimental flag, often with Irish emblems and slogans. Beside the US shield of red, white and blue, the 9th Connecticut's flag featured a golden Irish harp on a green shield, surmounted by an American eagle, over black-lettered gold ribands bearing the slogan *Erin Go Bragh* – "Ireland Forever" – above "9th REGIMENT C.V." (*History of the Ninth Regiment Connecticut Volunteer Infantry,* 1903)

Officers of Company E, 9th Connecticut, in a photo taken early in 1862. They wear dark blue forage caps with a gold bugle insignia bearing the regiment number in the center, dark blue nine-button frock coats with shoulder rank insignia, and black leather sword belts worn over red sashes. The officer in the center wears dark blue pants with a narrow sky-blue stripe, while his companions wear sky-blue pants (adopted by Connecticut troops in December 1861) with dark blue stripes. (*History of the Ninth Regiment Connecticut Volunteer Infantry,* 1903)

shoes, coats or blankets during that winter. Officers were better off, wearing the state's regulation dark blue kepis, frock coats, and pants. Connecticut began issuing US infantry clothing (dark blue forage caps, dark blue frock coats or blouses and sky-blue pants) to its troops in the spring of 1862. The first issue in May, as reported by Cpl John P. Coen, included dress hats with green tassels, green waist sashes, and green stripes on the pants.

Colonel Cahill was apparently somewhat lax in his record-keeping. On returning home at the end of the war, he discovered to his amazement that he had been dishonorably discharged for "disobedience of orders and neglect of duty," for failing to prepare proper muster-out rolls and records for the 9th Connecticut. The men had simply gone home, and Cahill had apparently provided no paperwork for them to sign. Fortunately for the popular colonel, public support caused the War Department to rescind the dishonorable discharge.

Illinois

The growing Midwestern rail and industrial center of Chicago became home to a large Irish immigrant population, and as in other major cities these communities formed volunteer militia companies. Organized in 1854, Capt James Quirk's Shields Guards, made up mostly of mechanics, was the first Chicago military company to offer its services to the Federal government in January 1861.

The 23rd Illinois Infantry Regiment ("1st Irish Regiment," or "Irish Brigade of the West") was organized in Chicago in June 1861. Colonel James A. Mulligan, an Irish-American attorney, modeled his unit upon the pattern of Col Michael Corcoran's 69th New York. The Shields Guards' Capt Quirk later became lieutenant-colonel of the regiment. The 23rd Illinois contained former Irish militia companies like the Montgomery Guards (Co B), Jackson Guards (Co C), Mahoney Guards (Co H) and Shields Guards (Co K), as well as the Detroit Jackson Guards (Co A) from Detroit, Michigan.

Following the Union defeat at Wilson's Creek on August 10, 1861, Confederate BrigGen Sterling Price led a fall offensive in Missouri, and on September 19 he defeated MajGen James G. Blunt at Lexington, where a large part of the 23rd Illinois passed into captivity the next day. Rather than surrender the regimental colors – a dark green flag with a gold Irish harp in the center – the soldiers tore it into pieces, each man receiving a small shred of the cloth. After being paroled the 23rd Illinois was reorganized early in 1862, and the regiment served in Virginia.

In the beginning, soldiers of the 23rd Illinois wore the dress of their individual companies and were armed with M1855 rifle muskets. Cook County furnished uniforms for the entire regiment: dark blue jackets with green facings, dark blue kepis, gray shirts, and gray pants with green stripes. In July 1861, haversacks and canteens were issued.

A second Irish regiment, the 90th Illinois ("Irish Legion") was organized at Chicago, mostly from Cook County companies, in September 1862. This unit contained five companies from Chicago, one from Rockford, and the remainder from other northern Illinois cities. Its commander, Col Timothy O'Meara (formerly with the 42nd New York Infantry), was a native of Tipperary; he had seen service in the US Army in Mexico during the 1846–48 war, and afterward on the Great Plains. The 90th Illinois was issued US regulation infantry uniforms, but officers wore green feathers in their dress hats. Arms were originally Austrian rifled muskets, then Enfield rifles in 1863, and Springfield rifled muskets in 1864.

Serving with Gen William T. Sherman's Army of the Tennessee, the 90th Illinois took part in his exhausting march from Memphis to join Grant at Chattanooga in November 1863. On November 25 the regiment went straight into action after a month on the road, and sustained heavy casualties during the attack on the Confederate right at Missionary Ridge; Col O'Meara was killed and several officers were wounded, among the regiment's nearly 100 casualties. The following year the regiment fought in the 1864 Atlanta campaign and took part in Sherman's "March to the Sea," as part of 3rd Bde, 2nd Div of Osterhaus' XV Corps.

Indiana

The 35th Indiana Infantry Regiment ("1st Irish Regiment") was organized at Indianapolis in December 1861; its companies were exclusively Irish, and hailed from Indianapolis, Madison, Michigan City, Lafayette, Valparaiso, Laporte and Delphi. The regiment saw hard combat in the Western theater. When Confederate Gen Braxton Bragg attacked MajGen William S. Rosecrans' Army of the Cumberland at Stones River (Murfreesboro) on December 31, 1862–January 3, 1863, the regiment lost 27 killed, 78 wounded and 13 missing. Colonel Bernard F. Mullen, a Mexican War veteran from Pennsylvania, com-

Cpl John P. Coen, Co F, 9th Connecticut, in an image probably taken at his enlistment in November 1861. He wears a dark blue forage cap, frock coat and pants; the trim on his pointed cuffs and down-turned collar is sky-blue. *(History of the Ninth Regiment Connecticut Volunteer Infantry, 1903)*

manded the 35th Indiana for most of the war. Major John P. Dufficy, an officer noted for his bravery under fire, was among those killed at Kennesaw Mountain on June 27, 1864, during Sherman's advance on Atlanta.

The first uniform furnished to the 35th Indiana was the dark blue nine-button shell jacket and sky-blue pants issued to the state's troops, but with a distinctive kepi of emerald-green, badged with a gold wreath of shamrocks and the numeral "1". This

Col James A. Mulligan, 23rd Illinois Infantry ("Irish Brigade"). A prominent Chicago attorney and politician, Mulligan was to Irish communities in the American Midwest what Meagher and Corcoran were to the Northeast. When he was mortally wounded in action at Winchester, Virginia, on July 24, 1864, his last words to his men were reported as "Lay me down, and save the flag." (Library of Congress)

7

1st Lt Bernard McCabe, Co G, 35th Indiana Infantry. McCabe wears the dark blue frock coat and pants typical of Federal officers; note the narrow light blue trouser-welt. The only item to distinguish this unit early in the war was a green kepi. (US Army Mil Hist Inst; Monmouth County Historical Assoc, Freehold, NJ)

uniform was replaced by US regulation infantry issue by the fall of 1862. The 35th Indiana was armed with Enfield rifles.

Men from a "2nd Irish" regiment that failed to materialize, Col Mullen's 61st Indiana, transferred into the 35th Indiana in May 1862. They also wore green kepis, but with dark blue chasseur coats with green trim, and dark blue pants. In the long run the standard US infantry uniform won out, although the regiment's Irishmen apparently clung to their green kepis throughout the war (unlike the majority of Indiana troops, who typically adopted black hats).

Maine

Organized at Augusta in December 1861 and mustered in January 1862, Col John McClusky's 15th Maine Infantry Regiment had a significant Irish presence in Cos F and I. The 15th Maine did duty on the Gulf coast, and served in the unsuccessful Red River campaign in the spring of 1864. The regiment had no known Irish distinctions of dress; it received US regulation infantry frock coats and kepis, and probably the dark blue pants favored by Maine regiments. The 15th Maine carried Enfield rifles.

Although not an Irish regiment per se, the 15th Maine carried a flag with a shamrock and harp on one side and the arms and motto of the state on the other. This flag actually figured in an early legal case of flag-related misconduct, when Col McClusky was court-martialed for conduct unbecoming an officer. Charged with tossing the regimental flag into the ocean while he was intoxicated, McClusky told the court that some of the 15th Maine's non-Irish soldiers had raised objections about fighting under an Irish flag, and that he had thrown it into the sea so that it would not be "dishonored, nor will it be a subject for dissension or dispute." Ruling that the flag was not an "official" regimental color, the court accepted McClusky's explanation and found him not guilty.

Massachusetts

Given Boston's large Irish immigrant population, it is not surprising that several Irish volunteer militia companies were active there during the 1850s. These included the Bay State Artillery, the Sarsfield Guards, and the mainly-Irish Columbian Artillery – uniformed in dark blue coatees and pants with red trim and black bearskin caps, and with a lineage as old as the American republic. A wave of anti-Irish, anti-Catholic prejudice erupted with the nativist "Know-Nothing" political movement in the 1850s, and consequently these Irish companies were disbanded by the Massachusetts governor, but many of them continued as social organizations.

The Columbian Artillery – which survived under the guise of a literary association – would be the nucleus for the 9th Massachusetts Volunteer Infantry Regiment ("1st Irish" or *"Faugh a Ballagh"* Regiment), organized in April and May 1861. Six Irish companies were recruited in Boston, and one each from Salem, Marlboro, Milford and Stoughton. Colonel Thomas Cass, the former captain of the Columbian Artillery, was killed in action in July 1862 while leading the regiment at Malvern Hill. The 9th Massachusetts amassed a solid service record with the 1st Div of V Corps of the Army of the Potomac, with combat at Gaines' Mill, Malvern Hill, Chancellorsville and the Wilderness. All told,

152 soldiers from this regiment died in action during the war, and 105 from wounds and disease.

The 9th Massachusetts was at first armed with M1842 muskets and conversions, but in 1863 the regiment received Springfield rifled muskets. Initial uniforms were the gray fatigue jackets issued by Massachusetts early in the war, but the regiment received US regulation infantry clothing in the fall of 1861.

The 9th Massachusetts was presented with an Irish flag that was carried by the regiment at Gaines' Mill on June 27, 1862, during the Seven Days' Battles. Of deep green, it bore an American eagle in the center with a shield of stars and stripes, supported by a wreath of gold shamrocks. Over all was a scroll with these words in gold: "Thy sons by adoption; thy firm supporters and defenders from duty, affection and choice"; and on the reverse, "As aliens and strangers thou didst us befriend. As sons and patriots we do thee defend." At Gaines' Mill the flag was carried by Sgt Jack Barry, who managed to come out of the slaughter unhurt, although ten color-bearers carrying the US flag were all killed or wounded. (This is a reminder of the fire attracted by colors, even on a day when their attackers – Field's Virginian brigade of A.P. Hill's Light Division – are usually described as being broken before reaching the Union lines.)

New York's popular Irish nationalist Thomas Francis Meagher spoke to an overflowing crowd in Boston Music Hall in September 1861, at a meeting intended to drum up Irish-American enlistments. Meagher, a powerful speaker, ended his talk with a rousing appeal to Irish patriotism: "Then up, Irishmen! Up! Take the sword in hand! Down to the banks of the Potomac!" A second Irish regiment, the 28th Massachusetts Infantry, was raised in Boston in the fall of 1861, and mustered into service in December. Colonel William Monteith's 28th

Col Patrick R. Guiney commanded the 9th Massachusetts after the death of Col Thomas Cass at Malvern Hill in July 1862. A native of Tipperary, Guiney regarded the preservation of the Union as "a cause bright and grand as the Sun." (Roger Hunt Collection, US Army Mil Hist Inst)

The 9th Massachusetts celebrating Mass in Camp Cass, Virginia, in August 1861; the priest was Father Thomas Scully, the regimental chaplain. Note the long-crowned "McDowell"-pattern forage caps worn by the officers. (Library of Congress)

Massachusetts ("2nd Irish Regiment") fought at Second Bull Run on August 29–30, 1862, with the 1st Div of IX Corps. Bundled backwards by A.P. Hill, the regiment had 28 killed and 86 wounded. At Antietam on September 17 they crossed "Burnside Bridge" to deploy in Benjamin Christ's brigade on the right of 1st Division's attack on Sharpsburg, and thus avoided the worst of A.P. Hill's counter-attack into the division's left flank. The 28th Massachusetts became a component regiment of the Irish Brigade (see below, under New York), which it joined in November 1862. At Fredericksburg on December 13 the regiment was in the center of the brigade's disastrous assault on Rebel entrenchments at Marye's Heights, and suffered heavily.

The 28th Massachusetts was issued regulation US infantry clothing and Enfield rifles, but its Irish regimental colors were strictly non-regulation. The first of four green flags, presented in January 1862, featured an American eagle and an Irish harp surrounded by shamrocks. Its second green flag, made by Tiffany & Co of New York City, resembled those carried by the other components of the Irish Brigade. Inscribed "4th Reg't., Irish Brigade", it was this color that the 28th Massachusetts carried at Fredericksburg. Early in 1863 the regiment received a replacement (believed to be similar to the first flag); and in May 1864 the city of Boston presented the 28th with yet another Irish flag; this one bore battle-honors, and may have been carried by the regiment during the 1864 campaigns in Virginia..

Missouri

Organized at St Louis in June 1861, the 7th Missouri Infantry Regiment was largely Irish-American at the start of the war. Known as the "Irish 7th," the regiment saw service in Grant's Army of the Tennessee (in 3rd Bde, 3rd Div of XVII Corps) during the 1863 Mississippi campaigns; its actions included Port Gibson, Champion's Hill and the siege of Vicksburg. There, on May 22, it played a leading part in the failed and very costly Federal assaults, planting its green Irish flag on the Confederate works until ordered to withdraw.

The 7th Missouri was issued regulation clothing and M1842 rifled muskets in 1862, receiving Enfields in 1863. The original green Irish flag was described in the *Boston Pilot* of July 12, 1862: it measured 6ft by 6ft 6in, and featured on one side the "Irish Harp, guarded by a savage-looking wolf dog, surrounded by a wreath of shamrocks, surmounted by the American eagle, and supported on either side by flags and implements of war. A golden halo shoots from out and over the whole. On the reverse is a 'sunburst' in all its glory, with the Irish war-cry for a motto – 'Faj an Bealac! [sic]'"

A second Irish-American unit, the 30th Missouri Infantry ("Shamrock Regiment") was mustered into service in St Louis in October 1862 and issued Enfields. The Shamrocks, like the 7th, also saw action in the siege of Vicksburg (in 1st Bde, 1st Div of Sherman's XV Corps).

Both Irish regiments dwindled in numbers as time passed, and in August 1864 they were consolidated into a demi-brigade called the "Missouri Irish Brigade," which served in the Trans-Mississippi. In April 1865 the amalgamated unit was present for the Federal assault on Fort Blakely, Alabama, the last major battle of the war east of the Mississippi.

New Hampshire

Organized in Manchester in September 1862, Col Michael T. Donohoe's 10th New Hampshire Infantry ("Irish Regiment") had a heavy concentration of Irish Americans in Co F and to a lesser degree in Cos B, I and K. The regiment saw service at Fredericksburg in December 1862 (in 1st Bde, 3rd Div of IX Corps), and afterwards in the 1864 Virginia campaign. Lieutenant-Colonel John Coughlin received the Congressional Medal of Honor for his conduct on May 9, 1864, at Swift Creek, Virginia, where he took the initiative and led his regiment forward (without orders) to repel a night attack. The 10th New Hampshire received regulation uniforms, and was armed with Springfields, although Spencer repeating rifles were issued temporarily for skirmisher duty in September 1864.

New York, before 1861

New York City's large community of Irish immigrants organized volunteer militia companies such as Brooklyn's Napper Tandy Light Artillery, described in the *New York Times* of March 18, 1854, in their shakos, green jackets trimmed with yellow braid, and sky-blue pants with scarlet stripes.

Until 1859 the dress uniform of the 9th Regiment, New York State Militia ("1st Irish Regiment" – reorganized as the 83rd New York Volunteer Infantry in 1861) was a black felt shako with white pompon (white plume for officers); a green coatee with white turnbacks and gold lace trim, and green epaulettes with white fringe; sky-blue pants with a white stripe, and black belts. In 1859 the regiment adopted a dark blue leather-bound shako with a red pompon, a dark blue frock coat with sky-blue collar and red epaulettes, and dark blue pants with a red stripe. The fatigue uniform was a dark blue nine-button shell jacket with shoulder straps, red slash cuffs and trim on the collar and shoulder straps, a dark blue forage cap with gold braid, and dark blue pants with a red stripe (changed to sky-blue pants in 1862). Overcoats were dark blue, and the unit had Springfield rifled muskets.

New York City's celebrated 69th Regiment NYSM was actually organized in 1851 (with three other Irish volunteer militia regiments) as part of a covert operation to train Irish immigrants to fight for the liberation of their homeland. The plan was discovered and the three other regiments were disbanded. The 69th's uniform until 1859 was a regulation blue dress cap with a red plume, a green coatee trimmed with crimson and gold, medium blue pants with a yellow stripe (white pants in summer), and black belts; officers wore a green-and-red plume. Prescribed blue coats were worn as a fatigue uniform. The 69th shed its traditional green coats in 1859, and adopted the dark blue caps and frock coats and sky-blue pants

Pvt John J. Bendon, Co D, 9th Massachusetts. A musician, Bendon appears to be wearing an untrimmed dark blue jacket and sky-blue trousers. His dark blue forage cap has the brass numeral "9" high on the front. (William J. Prince Collection, US Army Mil Hist Inst)

11

1st Lt James Fleming, Co B, 28th Massachusetts, wears a regulation dark blue frock coat and pants, the latter with a narrow stripe of light blue. Fleming entered the regiment as a first sergeant, and was eventually promoted to lieutenant-colonel; he was wounded three times during the war. (Dr Kathleen Dietrick Collection, US Army Mil Hist Inst)

of the New York State Militia. The coats were trimmed with red – the artillery color – because the 69th was classed as "Artillery doing duty as Light Infantry." For dress occasions red epaulettes were added to the coat, and a regulation shako with a brass plate and a green-over-red pompon was worn. The issue weapon was the .69cal M1842 Springfield musket.

New York, 1861–65

When the Civil War broke out in April 1861, the 69th New York, led by Col Michael Corcoran, became the second regiment to leave the city for Washington; it fought with distinction at First Bull Run on July 21, when Corcoran was taken prisoner by the Confederates. (Ironically, the first Rebel soldiers that the 69th encountered on the battlefield at Manassas were Irishmen of Maj C. Roberdeau Wheat's 1st Louisiana Special Battalion – the Louisiana "Tigers"). The flag carried by the 69th at Bull Run was a gift from Irish citizens of New York City – green, with a yellow sunburst, and red ribands commemorating the occasion in 1860 when Corcoran and his men refused to parade in honor of a visit to New York by the Prince of Wales; consequently, this came to be known as the "Prince of Wales flag."

The 69th mustered out after 90 days' service, but was reorganized as the 69th New York State Volunteers, which became the core regiment of the Army of the Potomac's Irish Brigade. This 2nd Bde, 1st Div of II Corps included four other Irish units – the 63rd and 88th New York, 28th Massachusetts and 116th Pennsylvania – and was commanded by BrigGen Thomas Francis Meagher. Formed in the fall of 1861, the brigade earned distinction as a hard-fighting command, and the 69th NYSV sustained the highest casualty rate of any regiment from New York. The three New York regiments were now wearing regulation US infantry uniform.

The Irish Brigade saw some of the bloodiest combat of the Civil War in 1862. At Antietam on September 17 the 63rd New York's colors were reportedly shot down 16 times, and both the 63rd and 69th NY suffered 60 percent casualties. At Fredericksburg, Gen Meagher gave instructions for the soldiers to wear sprigs of green box leaves on their caps to signify their Gaelic heritage. His brigade suffered enormous casualties in the failed second assault on the Rebel position behind the stone wall on Marye's Heights – 545 killed, wounded or missing out of 1,300 men engaged. Major William H. Horgan of the 88th New York was shot down at the head of his regiment just yards short of the stone wall. In yet another twist of fate, a number of the defenders in Thomas R.R. Cobb's Georgia brigade were Irish Americans, and the officer who commanded it, Col Robert McMillan of the 24th Georgia, was a native of County Antrim. When he spotted the green flag of the advancing 28th Massachusetts (the only one carried that day), McMillan is said to have brightened: "That's Meagher's Brigade," he told his troops; "Give it to them now, boys! Now's the time – give it to them!" The wounded lay out among their dead comrades all through the brutally cold night of December 13/14.

When Michael Corcoran returned to New York after being released from nearly a year of captivity, he was reluctant to share command with Meagher in the new Irish Brigade, so in October 1862 he formed his own Irish Legion. The nucleus was the 182nd New York Infantry (formed in part from the old 69th NYSM), joined by four other Irish units: the 155th ("Wild Irish Regiment"), 164th ("Corcoran Guard" or "Buffalo Irish Regiment"), 170th and 175th New York Volunteer Infantry. Seeing little action in 1863, Corcoran's Irish Legion was heavily engaged at Cold Harbor in June 1864, during Grant's advance from the Wilderness to Richmond. The 164th New York's Col James P. McMahon died while leading his men in a charge on the Rebel works on the first day of the battle, June 3; in these attacks the Union force lost some 7,000 men in an hour.

In 1862 Corcoran's Irish Legion was issued US regulation clothing and Enfield rifles, but in February 1863 the 164th New York received a distinctive uniform – that of "Hawkins' Zouaves," as worn by the 9th New York Volunteer Infantry. This unique uniform included a dark blue kepi or a fez with the numeral "164" and a green tassel, a dark blue jacket and trousers all with red trim, and white leggings. Officers wore dark blue

COL. MICHAEL CORCORAN, AT THE BATTLE OF BULL RUN. Va. JULY 21ST 1861.
The desperate and bloody charge of the Gallant Sixty Ninth, on the Rebel Batteries.

Col Michael Corcoran led the 69th New York at First Bull Run, where he was captured on July 21, 1861. The artist depicts Corcoran in a regulation dark blue officer's uniform, some of his enlisted men wearing red shirts and others stripped to the waist. He also shows a green flag with a gold Irish harp; actually, the "Fighting 69th" carried the "Prince of Wales" flag, with a sunburst motif, at First Bull Run. (Library of Congress)

Officers of the 69th New York, Fort Corcoran, spring 1861. They are dressed in US regulation dark blue frock coats, a mixture of dark and sky-blue pants with red welts or stripes of varied appearance, and dark blue kepis. Colonel Corcoran (far left) and a few others sport chasseur-type kepis trimmed with gold lace and a wreathed "69". (Library of Congress)

Officers of the 63rd New York pose with the regimental and national colors in 1865. The green Irish regimental flag, with a gold sunburst and harp in the upper canton, was emblazoned with battle-honors in block letters, including Fredericksburg, Chancellorsville, Antietam and Gettysburg. The national color has battle-honors in script lettering on its red stripes; these show that the image is not reversed, so the reversed lettering on the green flag must be showing through from the other side of the silk. (US Army Mil Hist Inst)

kepis, jackets and pants all trimmed with gold lace.

The 37th New York Infantry Regiment ("Irish Rifles") originated in the defunct 75th Regiment NYSM, an Irish unit that had been disbanded in 1856 but was reorganized in April 1861 and commanded by Col John H. McCunn. The regiment was originally issued the state M1861 blue fatigue uniform – dark blue forage caps, eight-button shell jackets, and light blue pants – and M1842 muskets (replaced by Austrian rifled muskets in 1862). The Irish Rifles also carried a green flag with a harp in the center, surrounded by a wreath of shamrocks, all in gold. A riband above the harp proclaimed "37th REGIMENT IRISH RIFLES", while one below read "N.Y. VOLUNTEERS". The 37th New York earned an excellent combat record in the battles of Fair Oaks, Fredericksburg (in 3rd Bde, 1st Div of III Corps) and Chancellorsville.

The 20th NYSM, later 80th New York Volunteer Infantry (Ulster Guard), fought in every major battle of the Army of the Potomac with the exception of Chancellorsville; at Gettysburg it was part of 1st Bde, 3rd Div of I Corps. The regiment was recruited in Ulster County, a coal and iron district north of New York City. One of the older component companies was the Jackson Rifles, an Irish unit formed in 1853 as a flank company of artillery, and uniformed in green coats (at first with buff facings and later with red). A regimental uniform was adopted in 1858: shakos with white pompons, dark blue frock coats with sky-blue piping on collar and cuffs, gray pants and black belts.

Officers of the 164th New York, "Corcoran's Legion," are shown wearing their distinctive zouave uniforms adopted in February 1863. While enlisted men wore the fez and jacket, officers opted for dark blue kepis, jackets and pants. Under magnification, gold lace trim is visible on the jackets of these officers, particularly on the forearms, as are the wide gold stripes on their pants; their kepis also sport gold braid. (Library of Congress)

The 20th NYSM served as a 90-day regiment in the spring of 1861 under the command of Col George Watson Pratt. This officer would be mortally wounded at Second Bull Run in August 1862, by which time the regiment was serving as a three-year Federal unit. Company F was overwhelmingly Irish as, to a lesser degree, was Co I, but every other company also contained 30 or so Irish names on roll. The 1858 regimental uniform was worn as a campaign uniform in 1861. An image of Pvt Benjamin J. Havenor of Co K, taken in spring 1861, shows him wearing what appears to be a dark blue eight-button NY state shell jacket with a standing collar and shoulder straps, and holding a dark blue forage cap. As a three-year regiment the unit was issued regulation uniforms and Enfield rifles.

Ohio

The Buckeye State contributed several Irish-American units. Irish volunteer militia companies – the Montgomery Guards (Co D) from Dayton, and the Hibernian Volunteers (Co F) from Cleveland – joined Col Alexander M. McCook's 1st Ohio Volunteer Infantry Regiment, recruited for 90 days in April 1861 and sent by rail to Washington. They were present at First Bull Run in July, but were only lightly engaged. In August 1861 the regiment was reorganized for three years' service, under Col Benjamin F. Smith. The 1st Ohio served in the Western theater; it fought at Shiloh, Stones River, Chickamauga (in 3rd Bde, 2nd Div, XX Corps), and in the Atlanta campaign.

Companies in the 1st Ohio left the state unarmed and dressed generally in dark blue forage caps, frock coats and pants (state militia dress, based on US Army uniform) or in civilian clothes. In May 1861 they received their first uniforms while in Philadelphia: dark blue fatigue blouses (similar to US Army sack coats), gray pants, red shirts, black felt hats turned up and fastened with a gilt bugle-and-eagle badge, and black overcoats. The following month they were issued US regular infantry clothing: dark blue M1858 forage caps with white havelocks, dark blue four-button sack coats and pants, and light brown blankets. Arms were "bright barreled" rifled percussion muskets. Enlisted men wore black cartridge boxes, cross belts and waist belts, with brass belt plates displaying "OVM"; canteens were covered with gray cloth.

Irish native Joseph W. Burke played a key role in organizing the 10th Ohio Infantry (Montgomery Regiment), an Irish-majority unit from Cincinnati, which fought at Perryville, Stones River and Chickamauga. An Irish flag, said to be green with a Maid of Erin in gold, was presented to the regiment in May 1861. The 10th Ohio was armed with M1842 muskets, exchanged for Enfield rifles in 1863, and wore regular US infantry clothing: dark blue kepis or black felt hats, dark blue fatigue blouses, and sky-blue or gray pants.

Pennsylvania

Recruited in Philadelphia, the 24th Pennsylvania Infantry was a 90-day organization that included the Emmet Guards, Hibernian Greens, Hibernian Target Company, Irish Volunteers, Meagher Guards, Montgomery Guards, Montgomery Artillery, Patterson Guards and

An unidentified officer of the 20th New York State Militia (Ulster Guard); this ambrotype was taken either before the Civil War or during the spring of 1861. He is wearing the regiment's campaign uniform: a dark blue frock coat with shoulder rank insignia, gray pants with a narrow welt of sky-blue, and a dark blue forage cap with gold lace trim and the wreathed regimental number. (Seward R. Osborne Collection)

15

ABOVE **Col Joseph W. Burke, 10th Ohio Infantry Regiment.** An Irish immigrant, Burke took command of the 10th Ohio after Col William Haines Lytle was wounded in September 1861. Burke's forage cap bears a gold wreath similar to the device prescribed for Ohio general officers in 1859. (US Army Mil Hist Inst)

RIGHT **1st Lt William H. Tyrrell, Co C, 116th Pennsylvania.** As a sergeant, Tyrrell carried the regimental flag at Fredericksburg, where the 116th Pennsylvania advanced on the left flank of the Irish Brigade; when he was hit by several bullets and dropped the shattered flagstaff, Lt Quinlan left the cover of a ditch to rescue the colors. Tyrell's survival of the freezing night after the battle is remarkable. He is shown here dressed in regulation infantry officer's uniform. (Mary T. Palladino Collection, US Army Mil Hist Inst)

Shields Guards (organized 1851). The regiment was mustered out in August 1861 after seeing little action. However, it became the nucleus for Philadelphia's 69th Pennsylvania Volunteer Infantry (Irish Regiment); Corcoran's renowned 69th New York was so highly regarded among the Philadelphia Irish that members of the new command purposely chose the same number as a compliment. The 69th Pennsylvania served in the Army of the Potomac; part of 2nd Bde, 2nd Div, II Corps, the regiment was conspicuous in repelling Pickett's Charge at Gettysburg on July 3, 1863, when their heavy casualties included Col Dennis O'Kane. The 69th Pennsylvania originally wore dark blue kepis, dark blue shell jackets trimmed with green, and sky-blue pants, and carried M1855 rifle muskets. Issued US regulation uniforms and Enfield rifles in 1862, it had Springfields in 1863–64.

The 42nd Pennsylvania Infantry Regiment (13th Pennsylvania Reserves, "1st Pennsylvania Rifles") was recruited in northern Pennsylvania in April 1861 by Col Thomas L. Kane. Company F, Capt Dennis McGee's Irish Infantry from Carbon County, came from a coal-mining area where the Irish secret society known as the Molly Maguires was active. Soldiers of the 42nd Pennsylvania were known as the "Bucktails" from their practice of wearing a deer's tail on their hats or forage caps. Their uniform was otherwise standard US issue; they received Enfield and Springfield rifles in August 1861, and Sharps rifles in August 1862. The "Bucktails" left a record of distinguished service with the Army of the Potomac; at Gettysburg they served in 1st Bde, 2nd Div of V Corps. Schuylkill County, coal-mining country to the west of Philadelphia, contributed three companies (F, I and K) with a high proportion of Irishmen to the 96th Pennsylvania Infantry Regiment. This unit, which also received standard infantry uniforms, fought at Gettysburg with 2nd Bde, 1st Div of VI Corps.

Following a rousing speech by Michael Corcoran in Philadelphia (in which he pointedly reminded his listeners that the underlying reason for enlisting was to turn out experienced veterans for a future war against Britain), the Irish-born Dennis Heenan, formerly lieutenant-colonel of the 90-day 24th Pennsylvania, raised the 116th Pennsylvania Volunteers ("Brian Boru United Irish Legion") in August 1862. The regiment joined the Irish Brigade that October; although badly under strength, it had an Irish-American majority. The 116th Pennsylvania received standard uniforms; initial armament included M1842 muskets, but in 1864 it had Springfields. Fredericksburg nearly destroyed the regiment, which lost so many men on December 13, 1862, that it was reduced to a battalion. Colonel St Clair A. Mulholland, wounded at Fredericksburg, led the unit until June 1864, when the entire Irish Brigade had become so small that it was led by a captain.

Vermont

Captain John Lonergan's Emmet Guards, recruited mostly from workers in the West Rutland marble quarries, joined the 13th Vermont Infantry as Co A when that regiment was organized in September 1862. Born in Ireland, Lonergan received the Congressional Medal of Honor for his actions at Gettysburg, where his company recaptured four guns taken by the Confederates, and went on to capture two more; the regiment formed part of 3rd Bde, 3rd Div of I Corps. The 13th Vermont received regulation uniforms and Springfields.

Wisconsin

Volunteer companies formed by Irish-American communities in the Badger State – the Mulligan Guards from Kenosha, the Emmet Guards from Dodge, and the Peep O'Day Boys from Racine – went into the 17th Wisconsin Infantry Regiment ("Wisconsin Irish Brigade"), organized in Madison in March 1862 under Col John L. Doran of Milwaukee. The 17th Wisconsin served in the Western theater; during Grant's defensive operations in fall 1862 it spearheaded a furious bayonet charge at Corinth on October 3, shouting the Gaelic war-cry, *"Faugh a ballagh!"* ("Clear the way!"). Later it saw service at Champion's Hill, Vicksburg, and in the Atlanta campaign. The issued clothing was conventional, and men of the regiment sometimes wore the black dress hat; the original Dresden rifles were replaced with Springfields later in 1862. The regiment carried a distinctive Irish flag (see below).

Col St Clair A. Mulholland, 116th Pennsylvania Infantry, a recipient of the Congressional Medal of Honor who had been active in Philadelphia's Irish-American militia units and who was wounded at Fredericksburg. He poses here in regulation US Army officer's uniform, complete with the red tasseled sash under his sword belt, but with non-regulation gauntlet gloves. (US Army Mil Hist Inst; Civil War Library & Museum, MOLLUS, Philadelphia, PA)

LEFT The 17th Wisconsin's green flag had a gold Irish harp in the center, above sprays of gold shamrocks. Gold-edged red ribands with gold lettering proclaim "FAUG A BALAC" at the top and "WISCONSIN IRISH BRIGADE" at the bottom; note that the triple-tailed tips of the lower riband also bear "Co" and "B". (Wisconsin Veterans Museum)

THE CONFEDERATE IRISH

Irish immigrants also settled in large numbers in the antebellum South. New Orleans, third largest city in the United States, had the largest Irish population in the Deep South, followed by Memphis, Tennessee; there were also sizeable Irish communities in Charleston, Richmond, Savannah and Mobile. The Irish were the largest single immigrant group in the South, and some 40,000 are said to have served in the Confederate army.

The Irish thought of themselves as loyal Southerners. Through determination and hard work they had carved out a niche for themselves in Southern society; Irish Catholics were more accepted here than in the North, were active in the dominant Democratic Party, and participated fully in political and economic life and military affairs. Many of them saw a parallel between the South's war of secession and the struggle of Irish nationalists against Britain. John Mitchel, Jr (son of an Irish nationalist immigrant who became an ardent voice for both Irish and Southern independence) commanded Fort Sumter in July 1864; mortally wounded in its defense, he is reputed to have said, "I die willingly for South Carolina, but oh that it had been for Ireland!" Patrick Cleburne of Arkansas – who became the best Confederate general in the Western theater – was a Protestant who recalled with equanimity his three years in the British 41st Regiment before emigrating; nevertheless, he would amply prove the sincerity with which he wrote: "I am with the South in life or in death, in victory or defeat." Many Irish Catholics in the South claimed that Northern abolitionists were hypocritical to condemn slavery while turning a blind eye to the treatment of Irish immigrant workers in Northern factories. More to the point, working-class Irish feared that an emancipated labor force of African Americans would compete with them for the heavy work on the docks, canals and railroads.

Caught up in the euphoria of secession fever, existing Irish volunteer militia companies quickly stepped forward to offer their services to the Confederacy, and new companies were raised. While the North fielded entire regiments of Irish Americans, the organization of Gaelic units in the South was confined mostly to company level. The Irish formed distinctive ethnic sub-units, which often performed skirmishing duties or protected the regimental colors. There were not enough Irishmen in the South to organize a whole brigade like Meagher's Union formation, but two Louisiana brigades recruited in New Orleans came close to this. The Missouri Confederate brigade that fought with the Army of Tennessee also contained a large number of Irish Americans, most from the St Louis area. Patrick Cleburne's division, which earned a reputation as the best formation in Bragg's Army of Tennessee, was not exclusively Irish but boasted a large number of Irish American soldiers. The 5th Confederate Infantry, recruited in Memphis, and the 10th Tennessee, organized in Nashville and nearby communities, were Irish regiments.

Alabama

By the outbreak of the Civil War the port of Mobile was a cosmopolitan center rivaling New Orleans on the Gulf coast, and boasting a large immigrant population. Several solidly Irish working-class volunteer companies were organized in 1861, but they served in different Alabama regiments.

1st Lt William L. Fagan, Co K, 8th Alabama Infantry. Fagan is shown in a typical Confederate officer's gray frock coat and pants, and carries a black hat. His coat has two rows of seven brass buttons, and under magnification can be seen to have light blue pointed cuffs, sleeve braid, and rank insignia on the collar. (Alabama Dept of Archives & History)

Members of the Mechanics Fire Company, nearly all of whom listed their place of birth as Ireland, formed the Emerald Guards in April 1861. On one side of their green flag was a harp encircled with a wreath of shamrocks and the Celtic war cries *"Erin Go Bragh"* and *"Faugh A Ballagh"*; on the other was the first national flag of the Confederacy, and a full-length figure of George Washington in the center. Led by Captain Patrick Loughry, who was killed at Seven Pines (Fair Oaks) in May/June 1862, the company joined the 8th Alabama Infantry as Co I (the regiment's color company) and served throughout the war in Virginia; at Gettysburg, for instance, the regiment – notably strong, with 477 enlisted men – served in Wilcox's Bde in Anderson's Div of A.P. Hill's III Corps. The Emerald Guards' uniform was dark green, although in Virginia they switched to eight-button gray shell jackets with dark-colored (possibly green) trim on the collars and cuffs. Companies C, E and H in the 8th Alabama also contained a number of Irishmen from Mobile.

Captain John O'Connor's Montgomery Guards became Co B, 21st Alabama Infantry in the fall of 1861, and spent most of the war as artillery in forts guarding Mobile Bay. Companies of the 21st Alabama at Fort Gaines in December 1861 originally wore red kepis (probably with a dark blue band and "a gilt bugle with silver 21 in the center" on the top); dark blue nine-button frock coats with sky-blue trim on the collars and pointed cuffs, following the pattern of Alabama Volunteer Corps regulations used by many new companies; and dark blue pants with a white cord (gray pants with black stripe for fatigue duty). Fatigue uniforms were phased in late in 1861 or early in 1862 – probably gray nine-button shell jackets with dark blue collars, pointed cuffs and shoulder straps, sky-blue pants and dark-colored leggings. Many officers continued wearing their dark blue coats well into 1862. Lieutenant-Colonel James M. Williams developed a fondness for the Montgomeries, of whom he wrote that they "stood heroically by my side in the battle of Shiloh" (where the 21st Alabama formed part of 1st Bde, 2nd Div of Bragg's II Corps). Williams wrote in June 1862 that "a new uniform for the entire regiment has arrived ... doubtless some home-made cotton stuff, but in this rough service that is just what we want." As the war progressed standard Confederate clothing became the norm; officers adopted gray frock coats, jackets and hats.

Captain Bernard O'Connell's Emmet Guards became Co B, 24th Alabama Infantry in October 1861, and a number of Irishmen also served in Cos A and H. The unit saw hard service in the Army of

Men of the Alabama Rifles – Co D, 1st Alabama Infantry – manning a mortar battery at Pensacola, April 1861. These men are mostly in civilian clothes, although the officer in the center foreground wears a "Jeff Davis" hat and a dark blue nine-button frock coat typical of Alabama volunteer militia companies. (F.T. Miller, *Photographic History of the Civil War*, 1911)

Patrick Ronayne Cleburne of Arkansas was the only Irish immigrant to achieve the rank of major-general in the Confederate army. This much-admired officer, called the "Stonewall Jackson of the West," was killed in action at Franklin in November 1864, during the ill-advised assaults ordered by John Bell Hood. (Library of Congress)

Tennessee; Capt William J. O'Brien, Co B's second commander, was killed at Chickamauga, where the regiment suffered no fewer than 200 killed and wounded while serving in Manigualt's Bde, Hindman's Div of Longstreet's Left Wing. The Emmet Guards' original uniform is unknown; clothing issued in November 1861 included gray jackets (probably the plain gray Alabama state pattern seven-button shell jackets with standing collar and shoulder straps, as issued in large numbers in the fall of 1861), pants, caps, Merino shirts and checkered shirts. The company received coats and hats in July 1862, possibly Columbus Depot pattern six-button gray shell jackets with blue collars and straight-cut cuffs.

Apart from those from Mobile a few other Irish units appeared. The Railroad Guards (Co B, 9th Alabama Infantry Regiment) boasted some 80 Irish former workers on the Tennessee & Coosa Railroad from Guntersville. The Alabama Rifles from Talladega (Co D, 1st Alabama Infantry Regiment) had at least 40 Irish or Scotch-Irish names on roll. Colonel William C. Oates of the 15th Alabama Infantry (a regiment of Law's Bde, Hood's Div in I Corps when it played a major part on the right flank of the attack on Little Round Top on the second day of Gettysburg) identified Co K of his command – the Eufaula City Guard or Eufaula Zouaves – as an Irish company.

The Alabama Rifles probably began their service in dark blue nine-button frock coats, and the 1st Alabama is known to have been issued dark blue frock coats, possibly with sky-blue trim, as regimental dress in July 1861; some of these were still being worn into 1862, although the regiment apparently began phasing in plain gray frock coats in the fall of 1861. The 9th Alabama may also have worn dark blue frock coats to Virginia in May 1861; while the 15th Alabama was issued gray frock coats, pants and forage caps with brass letters in November 1861, and their weapons were converted smoothbore muskets.

Arkansas

Irish neighborhoods in Mississippi river towns like Helena, Memphis and Vicksburg furnished manpower to a number of Arkansas commands in 1861. Captain Thomas J. Key's Helena Battery, a hard-hitting little company recruited in Helena and Memphis, boasted more than 50 Irish names, as did Co B, 2nd Arkansas Infantry (Hindman's, Govan's) from Helena. Company A of the 13th Arkansas listed about 40 Irish names from Memphis. Two Irish companies from Vicksburg, the Shamrock Guards and Swamp Rangers, joined the 18th Arkansas Infantry as Cos D and H. Little is known of the original uniforms of these units. In March 1862 the 18th Arkansas was in eight-button gray frock coats with dark blue collars and straight cuffs, and gray pants. This regiment later became the 3rd Confederate Infantry; it was consolidated in 1863 and part of 1864 with the 5th Confederate Infantry, an Irish command from Tennessee.

Neither Col James Fleming Fagan's 1st nor Col Patrick Ronayne Cleburne's 15th Arkansas Infantry contained any single solidly Irish company, but each had several companies with a strong Irish presence. These two regiments were consolidated into one during the 1864 Atlanta campaign; they served with distinction in the Western theater, from Shiloh to Bentonville. Fagan, the grandson of Irish immigrants, led the 1st Arkansas at Shiloh, where the regiment (part of 1st Bde, 1st Div of Bragg's II Corps) suffered very heavy casualties. In this command the El Dorado Sentinels (Co A), Clan McGregor from Pine Bluff (Co D), and the Ettoman Guards from Little Rock (Co F) all had at least 30 Irish names on roll, and in Cos G and H a number of Irish also appear. In November 1861 the entire regiment received new uniforms, "coarse but serviceable," probably from the state's clothing factory at the Little Rock Penitentiary: gray kepis, eight- or nine-button frock coats and pants made of gray woolen jeans material (sometimes described as butternut or coarse brown), with dark blue or black collars and cuffs. Light brown wool hats were also worn.

Patrick R. Cleburne, the former corporal in the British Army, was a successful attorney and druggist at Helena, and would become one of only two foreign-born officers to attain the rank of major-general in the Confederate army. His 15th Arkansas contained the Yell Rifles (Co C), his old company from Helena ("a splendid company of riflemen") with at least 30 Irish names on roll; the Napoleon Grays (Co D) and Phillips Guards (Co G) each contained about the same number. The Napoleon Grays was composed of many Irish riverboat men from the small port of that name, and earned a reputation for brawling and hard drinking. They often did duty as skirmishers, a dangerous job for which they showed a talent. The Napoleon Grays performed well at Perryville on October 8, 1862, where Cleburne ordered his Irish skirmishers – with regimental flags flying – to deploy ten paces ahead of his main battle line. As the Rebels reached the top of a hill, it appeared to the Federals to be the whole enemy battle line. The Federals opened fire, and Cleburne's main force quickly overran their position before they had time to reload.

The 15th Arkansas soldiers were probably first issued gray woolen frock coats from the Little Rock clothing manufactory, and forage caps, which were soon discarded for slouch hats. They were probably resupplied in the fall of 1861 with butternut-colored eight-button frock coats with black collars and straight-cut cuffs, butternut pants and wool hats. In the months after Shiloh the regiment received

As Confederate defenses crumbled on Missionary Ridge on November 25, 1863 – the second day of the battle of Chattanooga – Cleburne's division held firm on the northern end of the Rebel line. A number of Irish-American units served under the revered Cleburne in the Army of Tennessee; the soldier at the far right bears the distinctive dark blue flag with a white crescent moon carried by components of his division. (Library of Congress)

mainly Columbus Depot jackets – gray shell jackets with dark blue collars and straight cuffs. Flintlocks were issued at first, but by April 1862, when the regiment saw heavy combat at Shiloh (Cleburne having then risen to command 2nd Bde, III Corps), the 15th were carrying new British Enfields.

As Arkansas units gradually dwindled through attrition the Irish components in many companies also decreased. Unable to replace those who were killed, many regiments consolidated with others, and standard Confederate dress became commonplace. In June 1863 members of St John R. Liddell's Arkansas brigade in Cleburne's division of the Army of Tennessee were "well clothed, though without any attempt at uniformity in color or cut, but nearly all were dressed either in gray or brown coats and felt hats."

Georgia

Savannah was a major Atlantic port with a large Irish immigrant population, and this heritage was reflected in several militia companies raised there.

Formed in 1842, and named for Revolutionary War hero William Jasper (who was killed in the 1779 siege of Savannah), Capt John Foley's Irish Jasper Greens was one of Savannah's dominant volunteer militia companies, and the only one from Savannah to be accepted for service in the Mexican War. At the start of the Civil War the Irish Jaspers tried unsuccessfully to expand to battalion size, but a second company was formed in May 1861. The two companies went into the 1st Georgia Volunteers (Mercer's) as Cos A & B, and served at Fort Pulaski on the Georgia coast. In 1864 the 1st Georgia Volunteers was transferred to the Army of Tennessee, and during the Atlanta campaign Martin J. Ford of the Irish Jaspers became lieutenant-colonel of the regiment. The Irish Jasper Greens wore dark blue shakos with white feather plumes and wreathed "IJG" insignia; dark blue coatees with a single row of brass buttons, and green collars and cuffs; and dark blue pants with green stripes edged with buff. They later adopted gray Confederate uniforms, as did the rest of the 1st Georgia. Initial weapons were probably M1842 muskets, as this was the most numerous weapon in Georgia arsenals. The Irish Jaspers received a silk flag in August 1861: green on one side with an Irish harp and inscription "Irish Jasper Greens, 1842", and white on the other with the Georgia state seal and 11 gold stars. It is worth noting that when soldiers of the largely Irish 9th Connecticut were on occupation duty in Savannah in early 1865, the disbanded

An Irish company from Macon, Georgia, the Lochrane Guards formed Co F of the infantry battalion of Phillips Georgia Legion. This was among the units which stood firm behind the stone wall along Marye's Heights, from which Cobb's and Kershaw's Brigades of McLaw's Division mowed down wave upon wave of attacking Federals at Fredericksburg on December 13, 1862. (Library of Congress)

Irish Jasper Greens loaned them their Irish flag to carry in the St Patrick's Day parade.

Two other companies in the 1st Georgia Volunteers claimed an Irish heritage. The Republican Blues (Co C), formed as early as 1808, contained a large number of Irish or Scotch-Irish names. The Blues began the war in their fatigue uniforms – dark blue kepis, jackets and pants with white trim. The Irish Volunteers (Co E), a new company added to the regiment in September 1861, was described as wearing "service hats, jackets, dark pantaloons and waistbelts."

Other Savannah Irish companies included the Montgomery Guards (Co E) and Emmet Rifles (Co F) of the 22nd Georgia Artillery Battalion, stationed at Fort Pulaski in 1862 and at Fort McAllister when it was overrun by Federal troops in December 1864. Most evidence suggests the battalion wore standard Confederate artillery dress. The Montgomery Guards carried an Irish flag, presented to them by the Sisters of Mercy; this featured a large gold Irish harp surrounded by shamrocks, above the words "MONTGOMERY GUARDS".

Another Emmet Rifles company, raised in March 1861, became Co B, 1st Georgia Regulars; if they ever had distinctive dress or a flag, no descriptions have been found. Led by Capt William Martin (later promoted to field command), the Emmet Rifles received the state uniforms prescribed for the Army of Georgia in July 1861: "Confederate gray, single-breasted frock coats with Georgia buttons, black cords down the outer seams of the pants. Caps were gray." Gray jackets and pants were worn for fatigue; officers wore dark blue frock coats and pants and plumed hats. There was also a large Irish presence in this regiment's Company G.

Augusta contributed the Irish Volunteers, formed in 1852, which became Co C (the color company) of the 5th Georgia Infantry Regiment; this unit suffered heavy casualties at Chickamauga, serving in John K. Jackson's Bde, Cheatham's Div of Polk's Right Wing. The regiment received gray uniforms in 1862. Another Irish company from Augusta, the Montgomery Guards, became Co K, 20th Georgia Infantry; the Augusta *Daily Constitutionalist* of January 12, 1861 reported them in "showy uniforms" and carrying a "beautiful new banner."

The Lochrane Guards from Macon (Co F, Phillips Legion Infantry Battalion) saw action manning the stone wall at Fredericksburg in December 1862. An immigrant from County Tyrone, Capt Joseph Hamilton of Co E, commanded the Legion at the wall (all field officers being killed or wounded). By this date the Lochrane Guards may have been wearing Type II Richmond Depot untrimmed nine-button shell jackets with shoulder straps and standing collars.

From Atlanta came the Jackson Guards, Co B (color company), 19th Georgia Infantry Regiment. Company commander James Henry Neal later became lieutenant-colonel of the regiment, and was killed at Bentonville in March 1865. As the former 2nd Infantry Regiment of the Army of Georgia, the 19th Georgia was issued the state uniform of gray kepis, frock coats and pants with black stripes. A photograph probably taken in June 1862 shows enlisted men in gray kepis, gray frock coats and pants, and officers in dress hats with black plumes, gray frock coats with two rows of buttons, and shoulder rank insignia. An image of Capt John Keely of the Jackson Guards shows him wearing a more typical

Fierce in battle, if notorious for ill-discipline, Maj C. Roberdeau Wheat's 1st Louisiana Special Infantry Battalion was drawn from the New Orleans Irish community; the "Tigers" won renown at First Bull Run in July 1861. Here a drummer of the Tiger Rifles (Co B) is shown wearing the battalion's red fez, red-trimmed blue zouave jacket, red shirt and sash, and white-and-blue striped pants. (*Battles and Leaders of the Civil War,* 1887)

An impression of Irishmen of William Starke's Louisiana brigade hurling rocks at advancing Federals after exhausting their ammunition at Second Bull Run in August 1862. (Library of Congress)

Confederate officer's gray frock coat with two rows of eight buttons, collar rank insignia, light-colored trim on pointed cuffs (and possibly along the edge of the coat), sleeve braid, and a black waist belt with rectangular brass plate.

Louisiana

The largest Irish-American units in the Southern army came from Louisiana. New Orleans was a cosmopolitan metropolis with more than 24,000 Irish inhabitants – a quarter of the city's population. Although initially opposed to secession, the Irish volunteered in large numbers once it was evident that North and South would go to war. "As for our Irish citizens," John McGinnis' *Daily Delta* proclaimed, "Whew! They are 'spilin' for a fight with old Abe."

The Montgomery Guards had been organized in the mid-1830s, and the company wore blue jackets, pants, caps trimmed with yellow, and white belts. In January 1861 they received captured US arms from the Baton Rouge arsenal, most likely percussion muskets.

The Emmet Guards was formed in 1850, many officers being prominent Irish politicians; it adopted dress caps with green plumes, green coats, and sky-blue pants with gold stripes. Although Irish Americans composed 77 percent of this company, the Emmet Guards had only a 10 percent desertion rate during the Civil War – remarkable for any Southern company.

The Emmet Guards and Montgomery Guards both went into the 1st Louisiana Infantry Regiment formed in April 1861, as Cos D and E respectively. The 1st Louisiana was recruited in New Orleans, and at least a quarter of the regiment were born in Ireland; besides the Emmets and the Montgomeries, there was a strong Irish presence in the Orleans Light Infantry (Company F). The Montgomery Guards' Capt Michael Nolan, a County Tipperary native and New Orleans grocer, was promoted to field command and led the regiment at Antietam (in Starke's Bde of "Stonewall" Jackson's Div); he would be killed at Gettysburg.

Companies of the 1st Louisiana were dressed distinctively at first, but in September 1861 the regiment was issued a uniform by the state: eight- or nine-button frock coats, pants and caps. The first uniforms were blue, later becoming gray, and shell jackets began to replace frock coats when cloth became scarce. Belt plates were usually rectangular brass, with the state's pelican insignia enclosed by a wreath.

(continued on page 33)

ANTEBELLUM MILITIA – UNION
1: Columbian Artillery, Massachusetts VM, 1855
2: Captain, Montgomery Guard, 11th Regt New York SM, 1855
3: Corporal, 69th Regt New York SM, 1860
4: 69th NYSM "Prince of Wales flag"

PRESENTED TO THE 69TH REGIMENT

IN COMMEMORATION OF THE 11th OCT 1860

A

1: Sgt, Co I (Baker Guard Zouaves), 69th Pennsylvania Inf Regt, 1861
2: Cpl, 23rd Illinois Inf Regt ("Irish Regt"), 1861
3: 69th Regt New York SM, 1861

1: 1st Sgt, 35th Indiana Inf Regt ("1st Irish Regt"), 1862

2: Musician, 9th Massachusetts Inf Regt, 1862

3: Lt, Co B (Hibernian Guards), 8th Ohio Inf Regt, 1862

C

1: 164th New York Inf Regt ("Buffalo Irish Regt"), 1863
2: Sgt, 28th Massachusetts Inf Regt, 1862
3: LtCol, 63rd New York Inf Regt, 1863

D

ANTEBELLUM MILITIA – CONFEDERATE
1: Cpl, Co C (Montgomery Guard), 1st Regt Virginia VM, 1859
2: Lt, Co A or B (Irish Jasper Greens), 1st Regt Georgia VM, 1860
3: Montgomery Guards, 17th Regt South Carolina VM, 1860

IRISH JASPER GREENS 1842

E

1: Capt, Co C (Sarsfield Southrons), 22nd Mississippi Inf Regt, 1861
2: 1st Sgt, Co I (Emerald Guards), 8th Alabama Inf Regt, 1861
3: 2nd Tennessee Inf Regt ("Irish Regt"), 1861

F

1: Musician, 6th Louisiana Inf Regt ("Irish Bde"), 1862
2: Sgt, Co D (Napoleon Grays), 15th Arkansas Inf Regt, 1862
3: Cpl, 10th Tennessee Inf Regt ("Sons of Erin"), 1861

G

1: Capt, Co F ("Fighting Irish"), 5th Missouri Inf Regt, 1863
2: Sgt, Co F (Jefferson Davis Guards), 1st Texas Heavy Arty Regt, 1864
3: Cpl, 1st Virginia Inf Bn ("Irish Bn"), 1865
4: Flag, Co E (Montgomery Guards, 22nd Georgia
    Arty Bn

MONTGOMERY GUARDS

The most famous Louisiana Irish unit (and one of the most colorful and notorious) was Maj C. Roberdeau Wheat's 1st Louisiana Special Infantry Battalion (Wheat's Tigers), raised from Irish dock-workers in New Orleans. The unit fought well in July 1861 at First Bull Run (where they engaged the 69th New York), and in Jackson's Valley Campaign in the spring of 1862. However, Col Wheat was mortally wounded at Gaines' Mill, and without a commander of his caliber the battalion was disbanded in August 1862. Battalion companies were distinctively dressed at first, with the Tiger Rifles (Co B) in dark blue zouave jackets (faded to brown by the fall of 1861) with red trim, red shirts, red sashes, white-and-blue striped pants and white gaiters. Headgear included a red fez with a blue tassel, or a straw hat with a defiant motto written on the band. Other companies wore blue jackets, gray coats and red shirts. The battalion carried M1841 rifles without bayonets in 1861.

More than half of the New Orleans laborers who comprised the 6th Louisiana Infantry Regiment ("Irish Brigade") were born in Ireland; these included two of the regiment's colonels, Henry B. Strong and William Monaghan, both of whom were killed in battle – Strong at Antietam, Monaghan in the Wilderness. Richard Taylor, the regiment's first brigade commander, described the Irishmen as "stout, hardy fellows, turbulent in camp and requiring a strong hand, but responding to kindness and justice, and ready to follow their officers to the death." Companies of the 6th Louisiana were distinctively dressed at first, but their uniforms were becoming threadbare by August 1861 after just two months' service in Virginia. The 6th Louisiana was probably issued state clothing in the fall of 1861: long jackets and pants made of bluish-gray jeans material. As cloth became scarce the jackets or coats were replaced by shell jackets, usually trimmed around the edges, collar, shoulder straps and cuffs with half-inch-wide black braid.

Taylor considered the 7th Louisiana Infantry ("Pelican Regiment") to be a "crack regiment." One third were native-born Irishmen; predominantly Irish companies were the Sarsfield Rangers (Co C), Virginia Guards (Co D), Virginia Blues (Co I), and Irish Volunteers (Co F) from Assumption Parish. The 7th Louisiana received state-issued bluish-gray uniforms in the fall of 1861: kepis with light blue trim, nine-button shell jackets trimmed light blue on the collars and pointed cuffs, and pants. Lieutenant-Colonel Charles de Choiseul described it as a fatigue uniform "of a light blue heavy cloth, a very pretty and serviceable uniform indeed." After the capture of New Orleans by Federal forces in April 1862, Louisiana troops were forced to depend on Confederate Quartermaster depots for supplies. In Virginia they began receiving kepis and dark gray Type I Richmond Depot shell jackets with black trim on cuffs and shoulder straps.

From August 1862 to May 1864 the Army of Northern Virginia contained two majority-Irish brigades from Louisiana: William E. Starke's (1st, 2nd, 9th, 10th and 15th Louisiana); and Harry T. Hays' (5th, 6th, 7th, 8th and 14th Louisiana).

September 17, 1862: the bloodiest day of the war left the dead of Starke's heavily Irish Louisiana brigade littering the Hagerstown Road at Antietam. On the same day, Meagher's mainly New York-Irish brigade of the Army of the Potomac suffered heavy losses in an attack on the Rebel position christened Bloody Lane. (Library of Congress)

Besides the heavily Irish units already mentioned, every one of the brigades' component regiments had at least one Irish or majority-Irish company. The brigades were consolidated into one after heavy losses during the Wilderness and Spotsylvania campaigns of May 1864. Observing prisoners from Hays' Louisiana brigade in November 1863, one Yankee soldier was surprised by the quality of their dress: "better clothed than any we had seen before ... overcoats and jackets of a much better material than our own ... of English manufacture, much darker than the United States uniform."

In the Western theater, Louisiana units also contained large numbers of Irish Americans. At least a quarter of the 1st Louisiana Regular Infantry (raised in February 1861 in New Orleans) was Irish, with heavy concentrations in Cos C, E, F and G. This regiment served with the Army of Tennessee and suffered consistently heavy losses at Shiloh, Stones River, and Chickamauga (where it served in Govan's Bde, Liddell's Div of the Reserve Corps). Early in 1861 the 1st Regulars received a regimental uniform from the state: dark blue nine-button frock coats, dark blue pants with yellow cords and dark blue kepis, generally similar to the US dress uniform. Their fatigue dress included dark blue five-button shell jackets. Arms in 1862 were .58cal rifled muskets and .69cal smoothbore muskets.

In the 13th Louisiana Infantry Regiment, which also served with the Army of Tennessee, the predominant Irish companies were the Southern Celts (Co A) from New Orleans, and the St Mary Volunteers (Co G) from St Mary Parish. The whole regiment was about 25 percent Irish; organized in September 1861, the 13th Louisiana sustained heavy casualties at Shiloh (alongside the 1st Arkansas in 1st Bde, Ruggles' 1st Div of II Corps), Stones River and Chickamauga; it would be consolidated with the 20th Louisiana Infantry, which itself had four Irish companies from New Orleans. The 13th spearheaded Col Randal Lee Gibson's Louisiana brigade, a reliable formation of veteran fighters that was one of the last Rebel commands to surrender in 1865. Gibson's Louisiana brigade also contained partly Irish companies in the 19th Louisiana Infantry, 4th Louisiana Infantry Battalion, and 14th Louisiana Battalion of Sharpshooters.

The 13th Louisiana arrived in Columbus, Kentucky, in November 1861 without uniforms; the troops were to have new uniforms sent to them from New Orleans, possibly light-colored kepis with darker trim and gray shell jackets with standing collars, shoulder straps, and a single row of brass front buttons. An early-war image of John W. Labouisse, an officer in Co A, shows a zouave-type gray jacket fastened by 11 small ball buttons, with light-colored trim on the pointed cuffs, rank bars sewn on the down-turned collar, and full-cut gray pants with a dark stripe. This uniform could have been inspired by the six-company Avegno Zouaves (or Battalion of Governor's Guards)

Unidentified soldiers of Hays' largely Irish Louisiana brigade wearing gray "battle shirts" – a common item among volunteers at the beginning of the war – and gray pants with dark-colored stripes. They are holding dark blue forage caps. (Chicago History Museum)

that formed part of the 13th Louisiana; the Avegno Zouaves wore dark blue jackets and red pants. The 13th Louisiana carried Austrian and Enfield rifles.

Major John E. Austin's 14th Louisiana Sharpshooters battalion earned a commendable reputation as skirmishers, and its Cos A and B boasted at least 30 Irish names on roll. A surviving jacket worn by Pvt John A. Dolan shows that the battalion was fairly well uniformed even in the last few months of the war, when it was stationed at Spanish Fort near Mobile. Dolan wore a Department of Alabama gray shell jacket with a single row of five brass buttons, a standing collar of dark blue and an exterior pocket on the left. Dolan surrendered with this command at Meridian, Mississippi, on May 12, 1865.

Mississippi

There were Irish immigrant communities in river towns such as Natchez, Vicksburg and Port Gibson, and in railroad centers like Holly Springs in the northern part of the state. In the 9th Mississippi Infantry Regiment (enlisted March 1861, reorganized March 1862), some 60 or so Irish names – probably workers on the Mississippi Central Railroad – could be found on the rolls of Capt John P. Holahan's Co B (the Home Guards from Holly Springs), with smaller numbers in Cos D and E. The 9th Mississippi saw heavy combat in the Army of Tennessee (e.g. in Patton Anderson's Bde, Hindman's Div of the Left Wing at Chickamauga); Holahan was seriously wounded at Kennesaw Mountain in June 1864.

The regiment's companies (many of them volunteer militia) left home wearing their distinctive uniforms. The regiment was issued a uniform at Pensacola, probably in June 1861 but before February 1862: "long pea jacket coming well over the hips, loose pants – Zouave style – with Zouave cloth gaiters, caps with brass letter of company & brass figure (9)." This was probably a shell jacket cut longer than usual, color unknown, with loose pants, white gaiters, and forage cap with brass letters.

Captain William McKeever's Port Gibson Rifles (Co C, 10th Mississippi Infantry) boasted a strong Irish component. J.D. Edwards photographed the company in civilian clothes at Pensacola in April 1861, when at least one man appears to be wearing a forage cap and a dark-colored frock coat.

Unlike most Irish-American companies, which tended to be formed in coastal or river ports with large immigrant communities, the Jasper Grays (Co F, 16th Mississippi Infantry Regiment) came from Paulding, a farming community in the central part of the state. Captain James J. Shannon, a newspaper editor and the son of an Irish immigrant, raised the company and was promoted to lieutenant-colonel of the 16th Mississippi, which served with the Army of Northern Virginia (e.g., in 2nd Bde, 1st Div of I Corps at Chancellorsville). Companies A, D, & I also contained a large number of Irish Americans. Distinctively dressed at first, these companies later received standard Confederate clothing.

Capt James Lingan, 14th Louisiana Sharpshooters Battalion, was photographed in an officer's gray frock coat with two rows of brass buttons and gold lace rank insignia on the collar. (US Army Mil Hist Inst)

Missouri

Irish-American companies in St Louis formed part of the 1st Regiment, Missouri Volunteer Militia. The Washington Blues (formed 1857) sported bearskin caps, dark blue coatees trimmed with sky-blue, dark blue pants with light blue stripes, and white crossbelts. The Washington Guards wore shakos with a gilt eagle surmounted by "a gilt harp entwined with shamrocks." The St Louis Grays (formed 1832) wore black shakos with white pompons, gray frock coats with sky-blue facings, and gray pants. The Emmet Guards (formed 1857) wore bearskin caps, dark blue coatees faced with buff, and sky-blue pants with buff stripes; they carried a silk flag with portraits of George Washington on one side, and of Robert Emmet on the other, together with his quotation: "I have wished to procure for my country the guarantee which Washington procured for America." By 1861 there was a regimental uniform: dark blue dress caps, dark blue frock coats, and sky-blue pants.

Elements of the old volunteer militia went into the Confederate 1st Missouri Infantry Regiment, formed August 1861. Martin Burke, former St Louis Grays captain, became lieutenant-colonel of the 1st Missouri, one of the South's hardest-fighting regiments. The 1st Missouri served in Francis Cockrell's Missouri brigade; consolidated with the 4th Missouri Infantry, it won a glowing reputation in the Atlanta campaign, at Franklin, and on April 9, 1865, at Fort Blakely, Alabama – the last major battle of the war.

Irish companies in the 1st Missouri included the Suchet Guards (Co A), a solidly Irish company in fact from Louisiana; Co C (with 40 or so Irish, mostly from Memphis), and Co D (the St Louis Grays); the latter was commanded by Capt Joseph Boyce, who was wounded 11 times during the war. A wartime image of Boyce shows him in a gray frock coat with two rows of seven buttons, collar rank insignia, sky-blue collar and pointed cuffs, a waist belt with a round plate, and dark-colored pants.

Colonel James McCown's 5th Missouri Infantry, later consolidated with the 3rd Missouri, contained the "Fighting Irish Company" (Co F), which evolved out of the old Washington Blues. Under Blues alumnus Capt Patrick Canniff (whom Cockrell called "a fearless and skillful officer"), the "Fighting Irish" became one of the exceptional skirmisher units in the Confederate army. Canniff was killed in action at the bloody

battle of Franklin on November 30, 1864, during John Bell Hood's offensive into Tennessee. As the Missouri brigade prepared to assault the Federal works someone raised a roar of laughter when he quoted Admiral Nelson's Trafalgar signal – "England expects that every man will do his duty." "It's damned little duty England would get out of this Irish crowd," an Irish sergeant hooted. In Hood's impetuous attack the Missouri brigade incurred more than 60 percent casualties, the highest of any brigade at Franklin. Artillery support was provided by Capt Henry Guibor's Battery, a largely Irish company from St Louis; this was one of only two Confederate artillery units in action at Franklin.

Soldiers of Cockrell's Missouri brigade received new uniforms around the end of December 1862. These appear to have been gray caps and pants, and Columbus Depot pattern six-button jackets of gray wool, with collar and cuffs of indigo blue.

North Carolina

Two Irish-American companies in the 3rd North Carolina Artillery (40th North Carolina Infantry) served in the defenses around Wilmington, the South's last open seaport in 1865. Captain George C. Buchan's Co G (from Bladen County) and Capt Calvin Barnes' Co H (from Wilmington) helped defend the formidable Fort Fisher, commanded by Irish immigrant Maj James Reilly when the fort finally fell.

No distinctive uniforms are known for the North Carolina Irish artillery companies, which may have received the state clothing widely issued by North Carolina to her troops in the summer or fall of 1861. These were cadet-gray sack coats with down-turned collars, a single row of six buttons, and distinctive strips of cloth (red for artillery) on the shoulders; forage caps and gray pants with red stripes completed the outfit. They were probably armed with M1842 conversion muskets. In February 1862, North Carolina began issuing red-trimmed gray shell jackets, and by summer/fall 1862 untrimmed six-button gray shell jackets with standing collars.

South Carolina

Charleston had a large Irish community and Irish-American volunteer militia units that dated from the 1780s. The oldest, the Irish Volunteers,

Capt Patrick M. Griffin,
10th Tennessee Infantry, an
Irish immigrant who enlisted
in the "Sons of Erin" as a
drummer-boy. In May 1863 he
cradled the dying Col Randal
McGavock in his arms at
Raymond, Mississippi.
(*Confederate Veteran*, 1905)

received a green company flag made by the Sisters of Our Lady of Mercy and blessed by Bishop Patrick Lynch. The *Charleston Daily Courier* of September 12, 1861, described it as "made of the richest white and green silk, gold fringed, with eleven golden stars on each side, over beautiful wreaths of oak leaves, olive and the shamrock. On one side is the inscription, over all, of 'Erin Go Bragh.' On the reverse is the palmetto, embroidered in white, set off with golden spangles. In the right hand corner is the Crescent, and, above the palmetto, the motto, 'Et Presidium Et Dulce Deus.'"

As Co C, Charleston Infantry Battalion (1st South Carolina Infantry Battalion), the Irish Volunteers were stationed at Fort Sumter early in the war, and in other defensive forts around the city. They formed part of the Rebel garrison at Fort Wagner that thwarted a bloody Federal assault (spearheaded by the African-American 54th Massachusetts Infantry) in July 1863. After the Federals finally reduced Fort Sumter to a pile of rubble in September 1863, the exhausted Irish Volunteers were assigned to the 27th South Carolina Infantry for service in Virginia.

The Irish Volunteers traditionally wore green uniforms; the *New York Illustrated News* in February 1861 reported "two companies of Irishmen in green and silver" in Charleston. The dress uniform was probably a dark blue shako with green band and white feather plume, dark green coatee trimmed with silver braid, and blue pants with wide silver stripes. The company adopted a fatigue uniform in December 1860, probably forage caps, gray frock coats or jackets (possibly with green trim), and gray pants. By early 1864 they were wearing standard Confederate clothing and carrying Enfield rifles.

After the Irish Volunteers went into service with the Charleston Battalion, the remaining Irish companies in the city – Montgomery Guards, Sarsfield Light Infantry, Jasper Greens, and Meagher Guards (who changed their name to Emerald Light Infantry) consolidated themselves into the New Irish Volunteers (Co K of Col Maxey Gregg's 1st South Carolina Volunteers). The New Irish Volunteers became the 1st South Carolina's color company, and saw extensive combat in Virginia.

The New Irish Volunteers may originally have worn gray forage caps (possibly with palmettos and the numeral "1" above "S.C.V." and company initials), gray frock coats with green trim on the collars, and gray pants. Although 1st South Carolina Volunteers officers at first wore dark blue kepis, frock coats (with a single row of nine silver buttons, and shoulder rank insignia) and pants, the New Irish Volunteers' Capt Edward McCrady wore a gray kepi with an emerald-green band edged with gold trim top and bottom; he was still wearing it when he commanded the regiment at Second Bull Run in August 1862 (in Maxey Gregg's Bde of A.P. Hill's Light Division). M1842 muskets were issued in

June 1861. By 1862 most of the regiment wore gray jackets, pants and caps, with blue trim.

The New Irish Volunteers also received a distinctive company flag in September 1861. The *Charleston Daily Courier* described it as "rich white and green silk, with silver fringe, and eleven silver stars on each side. In the middle, on one side, is a Cross, with an Irish harp encircled by a wreath of oak leaves, palmetto and shamrock combined. Over the Cross is the inscription – 'In hoc signo Vinces'. On the reverse is a very handsomely executed painting of a palmetto tree with the rattlesnake coiled round its trunk – the whole presenting a very natural and life-like appearance. Around the palmetto is a wreath of oak leaves, palmetto and shamrock. Underneath is the inscription, 'Liberty or Death.'"

Tennessee

Memphis, the second largest center of Irish population in the Deep South after New Orleans, was home to a number of Irish units. Ladies of the city made up uniforms in the spring of 1861 for Col Knox Walker's 2nd Tennessee Infantry Regiment (Irish Regiment). An image probably made in May or June 1861 shows Pvt John Rulle of Co K wearing a dark-colored kepi with light trim, a dark eight-button frock coat with plain standing collar, light-colored pants, and a black waist belt with oval brass plate. The Irish Regiment was armed at first with flintlocks or conversion muskets. 1862 issues included jackets, pants, flannel shirts, canteens and haversacks.

Heavy losses suffered by the regiment at Shiloh (with Bushrod Johnson's Bde of Cheatham's 2nd Div, II Corps) led to its consolidation with the 21st Tennessee Infantry, which also included several Irish-American companies from Memphis. The result was the 5th Confederate Infantry Regiment, one of the most reliable regiments in the South. The 5th Confederate was a favorite of MajGen Patrick R. Cleburne, and it was with him when he fell at the head of one of the Rebel charges at Franklin in November 1864.

The 154th Tennessee Infantry, commanded during much of the war by Col Michael Magevney, included Irish volunteer militia companies. Memphis' Jackson Guards (Co C, organized in 1858) had adopted a conventional militia uniform: dark blue coat faced red, white pants, and a "West Point hat." The Crockett Rangers (Co H) from Memphis and the Henry Guards (Co F) from Paris were two other predominantly Irish companies. This regiment suffered heavy casualties at Shiloh (serving in Bushrod Johnson's Bde with the old 2nd Tennessee) and at Stones River.

There were also Memphis Irish in Co E, 2nd Tennessee Infantry (Bate's) and in Cos B, C (Montgomery Guard) and H of the 15th Tennessee Infantry (Carroll's). These two regiments experienced heavy losses at Shiloh, Chickamauga, Missionary Ridge and Nashville. Memphis Irish formed the nucleus of Capt William L. Scott's Artillery

Col Patrick T. Moore, 1st Regt Virginia Volunteers. The former captain of Richmond's Montgomery Guard, Moore commanded the 1st Virginia at First Bull Run, where (to the delight of his troops) he shouted the Gaelic war cry *"Faugh a Ballagh!"* (National Archives)

Battery, which fought to the last at Missionary Ridge before being overrun; there were insufficient survivors to re-form the unit.

Colonel Randal W. McGavock's 10th Tennessee Infantry Regiment ("Sons of Erin") contained Irish companies from Nashville, McEwen, Clarksville and Pulaski. The "Sons of Erin" carried a green flag with an Irish gold harp; they were issued gray caps, jackets, and pants with scarlet trim in September 1861, and were initially armed with flintlock muskets. A small but hard-fighting (and hard-drinking) unit that shrank through attrition, the 10th Tennessee saw action at Chickamauga (in John Gregg's Bde, Johnson's Div of Buckner's Corps), Missionary Ridge, in the Atlanta campaign and at Franklin. McGavock was killed in action at Raymond, Mississippi, in May 1863; he was succeeded by aggressive Col William ("Battling Billy") Grace, who was killed at Jonesboro in 1864. Major John G. ("Gentleman Johnny") O'Neill led the 10th Tennessee's efficient sharpshooter detachment before succeeding to command of the regiment.

Texas

The port of Galveston, the largest city in the Lone Star State, contained considerable numbers of Irish immigrants. On April 18, 1861, near Matagorda Bay, a Galveston Irish volunteer militia company called the Wigfall Guards took part in the capture of the *Star of the West*, a Federal vessel that had already been fired upon by Confederate guns in Charleston on January 9, when it had attempted to reinforce Fort Sumter.

The most famous Irish Texan command was the Jefferson Davis Guards from Houston (Co F, 1st Texas Heavy Artillery Regiment), a small company of mostly Irish immigrants that thwarted a Federal invasion of East Texas at Sabine Pass on September 8, 1863. Led by Lt Richard Dowling, the Davis Guards garrisoned a small fort guarding the entrance to the Sabine river. Through a combination of good gunnery and good luck, Dowling's men managed to disable two of the four Federal gunboats escorting the 22 troop transports, while a third gunboat ran aground, forcing the Federal commander to abort the landing. The Confederate Congress awarded silver medals to members of the company in recognition of this remarkable achievement, and authorized them to embroider on their caps "Sabine" enclosed by a wreath.

Virginia

The Confederate capital at Richmond was home to the Montgomery Guard (Co C, 1st Regiment of Virginia Volunteers), organized from the city's Irish immigrant population in 1850. In July 1859 the Montgomery Guard set aside its traditional green dress and adopted the 1st Virginia's new regimental uniform: black dress caps, gray frock coats with black trim, gray pants, white belts and

Lt John Edward Dooley of the Montgomery Guard – Co C of the 1st Virginia Infantry. This 21-year-old officer, who was wounded and taken prisoner at Gettysburg after Pickett's Charge, is shown wearing a standard gray frock coat with two rows of seven brass buttons. (National Archives)

gray overcoats. The fatigue uniform included gray kepis with black bands and gray nine-button jackets with black trim. The Montgomeries retained the green uniform for special occasions, and wore it when they paraded on St Patrick's Day, 1861; they also displayed their flag, the "stars and stripes, the first in a ground work of green surrounding the harp of Erin." The Montgomery Guard's former Capt Patrick T. Moore, a native of County Galway, commanded the 1st Virginia at First Bull Run, where the company was conspicuous in helping blunt a Federal advance at Blackburn's Ford on July 18, 1861. At this time the 1st Virginia probably wore a mixture of the regiment's gray frock coats and fatigue jackets, the Montgomeries in black 1858 dress hats ("Jeff Davis" hats). This clothing was soon in need of replacement, and in October the regiment received the familiar gray shell jackets that became so common among Confederate troops.

Capt George Horner, 1st Virginia Infantry Battalion ("Irish Battalion"), wears a gray overcoat and a forage cap with an oilcloth cover, with checkered civilian pants. Regarded as Confederate regulars, the 1st Virginia Bn became the Army of Northern Virginia's provost guard. (Courtesy Jim Ewart)

With the outbreak of war, Irish volunteer companies also appeared in the Alexandria area. The Irish Volunteers, an artillery company (Co C, 19th Battalion Virginia Heavy Artillery), did duty in the fortifications around Richmond. The Emmet Guards and O'Connell Guards went into the 17th Virginia Infantry Regiment in June 1861 as Cos G & I; this unit subsequently served with the Army of Northern Virginia (e.g. at Fredericksburg, in Corse's Bde, Pickett's Div of Longstreet's I Corps.) The Emmet Guards had adopted locally made green fatigue jackets and pants in May 1861, and (like other companies in the 17th Virginia) they wore their own distinctive uniforms until they wore out, probably by June 1861. They were issued altered flintlock muskets, but without cartridges or caps. Like other Virginia units, the 17th Virginia was eventually issued Richmond Depot Type II plain gray nine-button jackets.

A handful of Irish companies, recruited primarily from rail workers, formed in the Virginia mountains, but next to nothing is known about their uniforms. Charlottesville furnished the Montgomery Guards (Co F, 19th Virginia Infantry), while the Jeff Davis Guards (Co H, 11th Virginia Infantry) hailed from Lynchburg. In the famous Stonewall Brigade of the Army of Northern Virginia two companies were Irish: the Virginia Hibernians (Co B, color company of the 27th Virginia Infantry) from Alleghany County; and the Emerald Guard (Co E, 33rd Virginia Infantry) from New Market. There is a well-known account of the 33rd Virginia wearing blue uniforms at First Bull Run, when it helped turn the tide by capturing Union batteries near the Henry House. These could have been volunteer militia uniforms, but there is no record of the Emerald Guard adding any distinctions of their own.

The Emerald Guard were at first thought to be "unmanageable Irishmen" with a reputation for drinking and brawling. The devout "Stonewall" Jackson detached the company from the regiment in December 1861 and assigned it to temporary duty as field artillery. But the Emerald Guard atoned for its earlier bad conduct, returning to the

Grand Requiem Mass at St Patrick's Cathedral in New York City for the dead of the Irish Brigade, January 1863, from an engraving in *Frank Leslie's Illustrated Newspaper* of February 7. After Fredericksburg, horrendous casualties turned Irish opinion in the North against the war. (Library of Congress)

33rd Virginia in the spring of 1862; company commander George R. Bedinger wrote "I am very much pleased with the conduct of my Irishmen; they are enthusiastic and have at the same time obedience."

The 1st Virginia Infantry Battalion (Irish Battalion) was another command that had disciplinary problems. Four of the battalion's five companies were Irish, formed in Richmond, Norfolk, Alexandria, Covington and Lynchburg. After Maj David B. Bridgford took over the unit discipline improved, and the Irish Battalion discovered its forte – as the Army of Northern Virginia's provost guard, rounding up stragglers and guarding prisoners. The battalion did such a commendable job in its new assignment that it redeemed itself and earned a new reputation – as the "Irish cops" of the Confederacy.

THE EFFECTS OF THE WAR ON IRISH AMERICANS

In the North, Irish-American morale plummeted following the dreadful casualties suffered by the Army of the Potomac's Irish regiments in bloody engagements like Antietam and Fredericksburg. After the Irish Brigade sustained some 1,200 casualties in three major engagements between June and December 1862, Irish-American newspapermen began to question the use of Irish soldiers as cannon fodder; "We did not cause this war," complained the *Boston Pilot*, "[but] vast numbers of our people have perished in it." Irish recruitment dropped off sharply.

Other factors also contributed to Irish disenchantment. Wartime inflation in the North impacted heavily on unskilled laborers, many of whom were Irish. In the North as in the South, the abolition of slavery had never been popular among the Irish, who feared competition for jobs from free African Americans; Lincoln's Emancipation Proclamation, which took effect in January 1863, turned many of them against the war. As one Irish-American soldier wrote, "Indeed the spirit and patriotism of this army is dying out every day."

The event that pushed the Irish over the edge came with the introduction of conscription in the North; this smacked of discrimination against poor Irish, who – unlike wealthier Northerners – could not afford to pay substitutes to take their place in the army. Violence erupted in New York City in July 1863, as largely Irish mobs took to the streets in a four-day rampage of looting, burning and murder. Taking out their wrath particularly on African Americans, the mob left at least 19 blacks dead before Federal troops restored order; these riots also cost the lives of at least 100 Irish-American civilians.

In the South, postwar immigration from Ireland declined. Irish communities shrank noticeably, due to competition from the free African Americans who replaced the Irish in most unskilled work. These changes forced many who could not climb into the middle class to migrate West. Irish Americans continued to play a role in urban social and political life, however, and many of their old volunteer militia companies had reappeared by the 1880s.

The Fenian Raids

During the 1864 Atlanta campaign, Federal Gen Thomas W. Sweeny contacted Confederate Gen Patrick R. Cleburne with a proposal to join forces after the war, and recruit an army of Irish veterans from both armies for a war of liberation against Britain. Cleburne's reply was that once the war was over they would both have had enough fighting to last them a lifetime. Cleburne did not live to see the end of the war; but Sweeny did indeed take part in a Fenian "invasion" of Canada in 1866, as did hundreds of other Irish veterans.

The Fenian Brotherhood, a revolutionary group which was a forerunner of the Irish Republican Army, had formed in 1858, and even while the Civil War was raging it was aggressively signing up recruits from both Federal and Confederate armies. In 1863 Fenian cells sent delegates to the movement's first convention in Chicago; such revolutionary groups were also active in Boston, New York, New Orleans, Memphis, Savannah and Charleston. In the event two of the leading Fenian spokesmen, Michael Corcoran and Thomas Francis Meagher, played little part in this movement: Corcoran died in a riding accident in December 1863, and, amid renewed charges of alcoholism, Meagher fell from grace after Fredericksburg, resigned his command in May 1863, and drowned in 1867 after tumbling off a river boat.

In May 1866 the Fenians felt ready to launch raids into southern Canada (though with what realistic military objective, it is hard to imagine). Three raids were planned – from Chicago into Western Ontario; from Buffalo and Rochester across the Niagara River; and from New York and other seaboard cities along Lake Champlain – but only the

Fenian volunteers prepare for the abortive raid into Canada in spring of 1866. The movement recruited veterans of both the Union and Confederate armies. (US Army Mil Hist Inst)

The monument to the "9th Regiment Connecticut Volunteers" was erected in New Haven in 1903 to honor this Irish-American regiment, which lost 250 men killed or wounded during the war – one of the highest casualty rates in the state. (Connecticut Historical Society, Hartford, CT)

latter two were attempted. John O'Neill, a former US Army colonel, led an 800-man column across the Niagara River border near Buffalo in six vessels on the night of 31 May/1 June 1866, and occupied the town of Fort Erie. Already warned by the very visible gathering of Fenians at Buffalo, the Canadian authorities called out some 1,700 militia. On June 2 the Fenians drove back a small and incompetently handled militia force near Ridgway, inflicting 47 casualties in all. O'Neill then withdrew to Fort Erie, where a savage little firefight with 76 militiamen left 23 Fenians dead or wounded. The reinforcements that O'Neill had been expecting had failed to arrive, so he re-embarked to return to Buffalo; but he was intercepted by the gunboat USS *Michigan*, whose crew arrested the leaders and impounded their weapons. When O'Neill was jailed, Irish residents in Nashville raised $10,000 to bail him out.

On June 7 a force variously reported at 700 or 1,000 Fenians under BrigGen Samuel Spier crossed the border on the Lake Champlain route. Several British regular and Canadian militia battalions responded, and after two minor skirmishes on June 9 and 22 the Fenians withdrew.

In May 1870 "General" O'Neill – based at Franklin, Vermont – planned a raid into Quebec, but by the time it was launched on May 25 the British (who had long ago infiltrated the Fenian movement) had had three days' warning. The 350–400 Fenians were met on the frontier at Eccles Hill by a force of militia, whose fire checked them; when the raiders dragged up a field gun the militia advanced, and the Fenians fled. A smaller probe two days later was not pressed. By now internal divisions among the Fenian leadership were crippling the movement, which finally abandoned the romantic notion of capturing an Irish enclave in Canada.

SELECT BIBLIOGRAPHY

William L. Burton, *Melting Pot Soldiers: the Union's Ethnic Regiments*, Ames, Iowa (1988)

David P. Conyngham, *The Irish Brigade and Its Campaigns*, New York (1994)

Ed Gleeson, *Rebel Sons of Erin: A Civil War Unit History of the Tenth Tennessee Infantry Regiment (Irish)*, Indianapolis (1993)

Patrick R. Guiney, *Commanding Boston's Irish Ninth*, New York (1998)

Sean Michael O'Brien, *Irish Americans in the Confederate Army*, Jefferson, NC (2007)

Kelly J. O'Grady, *Clear the Confederate Way! The Irish in the Army of Northern Virginia*, Mason City, Iowa (2000)

Time-Life Books, *Echoes of Glory*, Alexandria, Virginia (1991)

Frederick P. Todd, *American Military Equipage*, 1851–1872, Vol. II, New York (1983)

PLATE COMMENTARIES

A1: Private, Columbian Artillery, Massachusetts Volunteer Militia, 1855

The Columbian Artillery's lineage dated back to 1789, but the company was disbanded in 1855 in the wake of anti-Irish hysteria. This private wears the company's black bearskin cap and dark blue uniform with red trim.

A2: Captain, Montgomery Guard, 11th Regiment New York State Militia, 1855

One of the many Irish volunteer militia companies that proliferated in the city during the 1850s, the Montgomery Guard was one of several (in both Northern and Southern states) to be named for Gen Richard Montgomery, an Irish-American officer killed in the unsuccessful assault on Quebec in December 1775. Irish companies were formed into several regiments in the New York State Militia. The Irish Volunteers wore shakos with white plumes, green coatees with white trim, and light blue pants with white stripes. A detachment of Lancers was decked out in czapkas with green plumes, green jackets, and sky-blue pants with yellow stripes. The Irish Dragoons wore crested metal helmets with white plumes, green jackets with gold trim, and sky-blue pants with white stripes.

A3: Corporal, 69th Regiment New York State Militia, 1860

The 69th New York was outfitted in the state's regulation dress uniform adopted in 1858. The dark blue cloth shako bore a green-over-red pompon, and a brass plate with the regimental crest (in this case Irish wolfhounds with the numeral "69" in the center). This corporal wears a dark blue frock coat, cut longer than usual, with crimson chevrons, epaulettes and trim; his sky-blue pants have a narrow crimson welt. The gilt waist belt plate is stamped "NATIONAL CADETS" (a nickname for the 69th) with the company letter in the center.

A4: 69th NYSM "Prince of Wales flag"

The inscriptions read "PRESENTED TO THE 69TH REGIMENT" and "IN COMMEMORATION OF THE 11TH OCT. 1860."

This unidentified member of the 37th New York State Militia ("Irish Rifles") wears a gray volunteer militia uniform jacket and pants, with dark-colored (possibly green) trim as blind buttonholes on the collar, probably on the shoulder straps, as three-button cuff flaps, and in broad stripes on the trousers. (US Army Mil Hist Inst)

B1: Sergeant, Company I (Baker Guard Zouaves), 69th Pennsylvania Infantry Regiment, 1861

Two zouave companies, the Tiger Zouaves and Baker Guard Zouaves (named for Col Edward D. Baker, the brigade commander killed in his disastrous action at Ball's Bluff, Virginia), were attached to this regiment in October 1861. Serving as flanking companies, they wore blue zouave jackets trimmed with green, sky-blue vests and full-cut pants, and blue kepis. This plate is based on an image of Lt Anthony McDermott of Company I.

B2: Corporal, 23rd Illinois Infantry Regiment ("Irish Regiment"), 1861

This distinctive uniform was issued by Cook County to the 23rd Illinois when the regiment was organized in June 1861; green trim on the dark blue shell jackets and green stripes on the gray pants provided the Gaelic touches. After the regiment was reorganized in January 1862, the 23rd Illinois was issued the state blue fatigue uniform (dark blue kepis, dark blue nine-button shell jackets, and sky-blue pants); and after July 1862, the troops adopted US regular infantry uniforms. Both Enfield rifles and Henry repeating rifles were issued.

B3: Private, 69th Regiment New York State Militia, 1861

The "Fighting Sixty-Ninth" was enlisted for 90 days' service at the start of the Civil War, and established a solid reputation for itself at the First Battle of Bull Run in July 1861. Enlisted men went into battle wearing a mixture of straw hats, dark blue kepis (with or without white havelocks), and dark blue state fatigue jackets with red trim. In the extreme heat, many discarded their jackets and fought in their red or gray flannel shirts and sky-blue pants. One company (Co K, Meagher's Zouaves) wore dark blue kepis, dark blue jackets with red lace, light blue pants, and a green sash.

C1: First Sergeant, 35th Indiana Infantry Regiment ("1st Irish Regiment"), 1862

The senior NCO of his company wears the dark green kepi with gold shamrock wreath that distinguished this Irish Hoosier regiment; otherwise, his uniform is typical of early-war Indiana units. The regiment's distinctive Irish flag **(inset)** was presented to the 35th Indiana in December 1861.

C2: Musician, 9th Massachusetts Infantry Regiment, 1862

The 9th Massachusetts initially received the gray fatigue jackets issued by the state to its regiments early in the war. Most (if not all) of the gray flannel blouses or jackets were edged with red lace;

light gray felt hats and gray overcoats were also issued. US regulation infantry clothing arrived in the fall of 1861, but musicians in the regiment continued wearing gray jackets, pants and caps.

C3: Lieutenant, Company B (Hibernian Guards), 8th Ohio Infantry Regiment, 1862

Captain William Kenney's Hibernian Guards from Cleveland became Co B, 8th Ohio, organized in May 1861. Issued regular US infantry clothing, the Hibernians were assigned as skirmishers for the regiment and were armed with Enfield rifles. They left a record of distinguished service with the Army of the Potomac; the 8th Ohio sustained close to 50 percent casualties at Antietam, fighting at the Sunken Road, and at Gettysburg they helped to repulse Pickett's Charge. An image of Capt James K. O'Reilly of Co B provided the model for this plate.

D1: Private, 164th New York Infantry Regiment ("Buffalo Irish Regiment"), 1863

Recruited from the town of Buffalo, the 164th New York received the Hawkins' Zouaves uniform of the 9th New York in February 1863 and, unlike most zouave units, continued wearing it until late in the war. The green tassel on the dark blue fez distinguished them as an Irish command.

D2: Sergeant, 28th Massachusetts Infantry Regiment, 1862

The 28th Massachusetts was the only Irish Brigade regiment to carry its green flag into the attack on Marye's Heights at Fredericksburg on December 13, 1862; the Gaelic inscription "*riam nar dhruid o shairn lann*" translates as "Who Never Retreated from the Clash of Spears." Leading the brigade's attack on the stone wall, the 28th Massachusetts lost 158 men killed and wounded out of 416 – the greatest number of casualties it would lose in a single day during the war. The Irish Brigade wore greatcoats during the attack, but dumped their packs; to distinguish them as Irish, they were instructed to wear sprigs of green box leaves on their caps.

D3: Lieutenant-Colonel, 63rd New York Infantry Regiment, 1863

A component of the Irish Brigade, the 63rd New York wore regulation US infantry uniforms, although soldiers of this regiment seemed to prefer black felt hats over the forage cap. The 63rd New York carried the same flag as the 69th New York. The red shamrock on

Dark blue frock coat of the 20th NYSM, as adopted by the regiment in 1858 and worn (minus the shoulder scales) in the early months of the Civil War as a campaign uniform. The buttons are those of the Ulster Guard, and the piping on the edges of the collar and pointed cuffs is sky-blue. (Seward R. Osborne Collection)

this officer's hat signifies that the Irish Brigade was part of the Army of the Potomac's II Corps; such corps badges came into use in the spring of 1863.

E1: Corporal, Company C (Montgomery Guard), 1st Regiment Virginia Volunteer Militia, 1859

The dress uniform of this Richmond militia company was spelled out in detail in 1850. The green-over-buff pompon on the shako was often replaced by a white feather plume. The Montgomery Guard, formed by Irish immigrants, was one of the most dependable companies in the 1st Virginia Infantry.

E2: Lieutenant, Company A or B (Irish Jasper Greens), 1st Regiment Georgia Volunteer Militia, 1860

This Savannah company dated from 1842 **(see flag, inset)**, and its original uniforms were green coats and pants with buff facings and trim. Later the Irish Jaspers adopted blue coatees with green trim, and pants were dark blue with green stripes edged in buff. Officers of several pre-war militias wore sleeve chevrons. The fatigue uniform substituted dark blue kepis with a green cap band and "IJG" insignia, and dark blue ten-button shell jackets with shoulder straps, green collars and pointed cuffs. Buttons featured an Irish harp surmounted by an eagle and the initials "IJG"; belts were black, with oval plates bearing the "IJG" cypher.

E3: Private, Montgomery Guards, 17th Regiment South Carolina Volunteer Militia, 1860

A component of Charleston's volunteer militia, the Montgomery Guards was organized in 1860 under Capt James Conner, later a brigadier-general wounded at Gaines' Mill. A fatigue uniform adopted in December 1860 consisted of kepis, gray frock coats or jackets and pants with green trim. The dress uniform was a dark blue cloth shako with dark green band, brass eagle cap badge above the initials "M.G." and a white cock's-feather plume; a dark green single-breasted coatee with three rows of nine white metal front buttons, and two silver braid buttonholes on each side of the collar; and light blue pants with a 1½in silver stripe.

F1: Captain, Company C (Sarsfield Southrons), 22nd Mississippi Infantry Regiment, 1861

Captain Felix Hughes, a prominent Irish immigrant planter, raised this Vicksburg company, which later fought at Shiloh. The company's flag was a First National pattern with a golden harp in the center bar, surrounded by dark green magnolia tree leaves and white magnolia flowers. Inscribed on white scrolls in gold letters were "Vicksburg", "Sarsfield Southrons", and "Faugh A Ballagh." Hughes, in temporary command of the 22nd Mississippi, was killed in action at Baton Rouge on August 5, 1862. There was also a strong Irish

presence in Companies D & I of this regiment. This plate is based on a portrait of Hughes now in the Old Court House Museum, Vicksburg.

F2: First Sergeant, Company I (Emerald Guards), 8th Alabama Infantry Regiment, 1861
Formed from Irish members of a volunteer fire company in Mobile, the Emerald Guards became the color company for the 8th Alabama, a unit which saw intense combat with the Army of Northern Virginia. They left the Gulf City carrying a distinctive Irish green flag and dressed in green uniforms, which they exchanged for gray jackets with green trim in Virginia. The Emerald Guards' captain, Patrick Loughry, was cut down at Seven Pines during the Peninsula campaign of May/June 1862.

F3: Private, 2nd Tennessee Infantry Regiment ("Irish Regiment"), 1861
With Irish-American companies like the Emerald Guards (Co H) and the Carroll Guards (Co I), Memphis made considerable efforts at the beginning of the war to provide clothing for the city's troops. Local women's aid societies supplied uniforms to practically all the new volunteer companies through the summer months of 1861, until the state quartermaster department was up and running. These initial uniforms quickly wore out, and the state began furnishing clothing in the fall of 1861. Like a number of other units, the 2nd Tennessee probably received grayish-brown ("butternut") nine-button frock coats with black collars and pointed cuffs with a distinctive arrangement of buttons; grayish-brown pants with black stripes; and gray forage caps with black bands.

G1: Musician, 6th Louisiana Infantry Regiment ("Irish Brigade"), 1862
Over half the soldiers in this regiment were Irish-born. Distinctively dressed at first, companies went through their first issue of clothing fairly quickly, and they probably received state clothing in the fall of 1861. Richard Taylor described his brigade in early 1862 as wearing "fresh clothing of gray with white gaiters." This musician wears a Richmond Depot Type I shell jacket, issued to many units in the Army of Northern Virginia in 1862.

G2: Sergeant, Company D (Napoleon Grays), 15th Arkansas Infantry Regiment, 1862
Rough-hewn Irish riverboat men from the boisterous Mississippi river town of Napoleon, Arkansas, dominated this company in the 15th Arkansas, led by "Old Pat" Cleburne before he rose to command first a brigade, and then a division. They became one of his most dependable skirmisher companies, seeing heavy combat at Shiloh and Perryville. Their gray shell jackets were of Columbus Depot Type I pattern, and their sky-blue trousers and Federal accoutrements came to them by the capture of US supplies at Richmond, Kentucky.

G3: Corporal, 10th Tennessee Infantry Regiment ("Sons of Erin"), 1861
Colonel Randal W. McGavock, the mayor of Nashville, purchased uniforms for men of his regiment in September 1861: gray kepis, jackets and pants, all with scarlet trim. The unit's green flag (inset) featured a gold Irish harp, with the inscriptions "Sons of Erin" and "Go Where Glory Waits You." The Sons of Erin were initially armed with flintlocks.

H1: Captain, Company F ("Fighting Irish Company"), 5th Missouri Infantry Regiment, 1863
The Missouri brigade received new uniforms in late December 1862, and members of this outstanding skirmisher company began the New Year in gray caps, gray jackets with light blue trim, and gray pants. They would trade in their Springfields for Enfield rifles in May 1863. Officers were dressed in standard Confederate infantry frock coats. A portrait of the much-wounded Missouri brigade officer Capt Joseph Boyce provides the model for this plate.

H2: Sergeant, Company F (Jefferson Davis Guards), 1st Texas Heavy Artillery Regiment, 1864
This sergeant in Lt Richard Dowling's Davis Guards examines the silver medal awarded to members of the company by the Confederate Congress for "one of the most brilliant and heroic achievements in the history of this war" – their defense of Sabine Pass. The company's standard artillery caps and frock coats came from the Houston clothing depot.

H3: Corporal, 1st Virginia Infantry Battalion ("Irish Battalion"), 1865
During the Army of Northern Virginia's hard-pressed retreat west from Petersburg in April 1865, this corporal wears captured US equipment with his gray jacket and pants, part of the extensive shipments of clothing received by Lee's army from Peter Tait & Co of Limerick, Ireland. The Irish Battalion served as the provost guard for the Army of Northern Virginia.

H4: Flag, Company E, (Montgomery Guards), 22nd Georgia Artillery Battalion
This cross-pole flag, presented by the Sisters of Mercy and carried at Fort Pulaski in March 1862, measured 36in x 49in, with 4in gold fringes.

INDEX